76553

THE BARRYTOWN TRILOGY

79

D1079699

Ireland Into Film

Series editors:
Keith Hopper (text) and Gráinne Humphreys (images)

Ireland Into Film is the first project in a number of planned collaborations between Cork University Press and the Irish Film Institute. The general aim of this publishing initiative is to increase the critical understanding of 'Irish' Film (i.e. films made in, or about, Ireland). This particular series brings together writers and scholars from the fields of Film and Literary Studies to examine notable adaptations of Irish literary texts.

Other titles available in this series:

The Dead (Kevin Barry)
December Bride (Lance Pettitt)
This Other Eden (Fidelma Farley)
The Informer (Patrick F. Sheeran)
The Quiet Man (Luke Gibbons)
The Field (Cheryl Temple Herr)
Dancing at Lughnasa (Joan FitzPatrick Dean)
Ulysses (Margot Norris)
Nora (Gerardine Meaney)
Felicia's Journey (Stephanie McBride)

Forthcoming:

The Butcher Boy (Colin MacCabe)

Ireland Into Film

THE BARRYTOWN TRIOLGY

Michael Cronin

CORK **cup** UNIVERSITY PRESS

in association with
THE IRISH FILM INSTITUTE

First published in 2006 by
Cork University Press
Cork
Ireland

British Library Cataloguing in Publication Data
A CIP catalogue record for this book is available from the British Library.

ISBN-10: 1-85918-404-9
ISBN-13: 978-1-85918-404-2

Typesetting by Red Barn Publishing, Skeagh, Skibbereen

Printed by ColourBooks Ltd, Baldoyle, Dublin

Ireland Into Film receives financial assistance from
the Arts Council/An Chomhairle Ealaíon and the Irish Film Institute

For Máirtín

CONTENTS

LIST OF ILLUSTRATIONS

Acknowledgements

I am grateful to Keith Hopper for his patience and forbearance as I worked on the volume. His commitment and enthusiasm were important at all times. I would also like to thank the library staff of Dublin City University, the National Library of Ireland and the Bibliothèque Nationale de France. I would like to thank the staff of the Irish Film Archive of the Irish Film Institute for their generous assistance in seeking out materials and, in particular, the Assistant Director, Gráinne Humphreys, for her help in sourcing images. Completion of the volume was greatly facilitated by the granting of sabbatical leave for the academic year 2004–2005, for which I am grateful to the Governing Authority of Dublin City University. My colleagues in two northside institutions, Dublin City University and St Patrick's College, Drumcondra, have been a constant source of stimulus and encouragement as I worked on the publication and I would like to take this opportunity to thank them for their continuing support. As always Máirtín Cronin has been a peerless companion and I dedicate this book to the ex-Snapper with Commitment.

The editors would also like to thank Sharon McGarry, Twentieth Century Fox, Alexei Boltho, BBC Films, Ben Cloney, Deirdre Dolan, Kazandra O'Connell and the staff of the Irish Film Archive, Seán Ryder and Sara Wilbourne.

1

THE BARRYTOWN TRILOGY: INTRODUCTION

If Ireland has gone into film, there have probably been few contemporary Irish writers who have been so closely identified with the enterprise as Roddy Doyle. Indeed, for some, the real plot in Roddy Doyle's work has been the plot on cinema itself. In an interview with Liam Fay published in *Hot Press* in 1993, Roddy Doyle expressed his surprise at the peculiarly Irish form of the hermeneutics of suspicion which saw his writing as essentially a cynical manoeuvre to seduce the moguls of celluloid: 'There was all this stuff about how I had written *The Van* with a view to selling it as a screenplay, that it wasn't a novel at all and that I had my eye on the Hollywood market. Leaving aside the actual content of the book – two middle-aged men with a chip van – it was still baffling.'[1] Doyle is right to be sceptical about the motives of his more malign critics, but he should be less baffled that his work is associated with an artistic practice that has been an integral part not only of the lives of his characters but of his own activity as a writer. In this study we will be concentrating on a high point of that activity, namely the film versions of three novels which constitute the Barrytown Trilogy, which appeared as *The Commitments* (1991), *The Snapper* (1993) and *The Van* (1996). Taken together, the novels and the films constitute a crucial body of work that not only gives voice to the particular preoccupations of the recent Irish past but that remains startlingly contemporary in the manner in which it articulates the specific relationship between Irish locality and global futures. In this chapter we will elaborate on a series of contexts for the Barrytown Trilogy and its journey into film, before dealing with each specific film, in turn, in the succeeding chapters.

When James Joyce built his city in fiction, he was not to know that after independence the literary construction crews would leave the city and take up residence in the countryside and on the offshore islands of the Celtic Fringe.[2] The reasons for the desertion were various. Firstly, the Irish Literary Renaissance which would gradually provide the cultural alibi for political nationalism was strongly influenced by a Romantic disdain for the satanic mills of the metropolis. Secondly, the economy which emerged after independence and partition no longer had the industrial bastion of the north-east nor the ready markets of Empire as protectionism began to take hold on Irish trade. The result was that the Free State economy remained heavily dependent on agriculture for its economic well-being.[3] Thirdly, the cities, as the memorials of the invader, whether Viking, Norman or English, were viewed as alien to the authentic, Gaelic spirit of the nation which was deemed to find its natural expression in the finely honed lyric of the smallholding or the epic biographies of the Western Isle. Fourthly, as early as 1925 with the establishment of the Irish Travel Association, the State became involved with the promotion of Ireland as a tourist destination. The image of Ireland conveyed by the tourist industry was almost exclusively rural, with a premium placed on quaintness as a guarantor of the authentic and the exotic.[4] The fact that much of the ruralist mythmaking was the production of an urban intelligentsia was largely ignored, as was the rural misery that gives lie to the easy sentimentalism of metropolitan idealisation. Indeed, not only would the city disappear from view but so also would those inhabitants who had not the good literary fortune to be born into the lower and upper middle class in the new state. By the late 1920s two of the primary literary voices of Irish urban experience, writing from a variety of class perspectives, Joyce and O'Casey, had gone into exile. Irish cities themselves did not experience any significant growth for several decades and agriculture continued to be the mainstay of Irish economic life. The changes prompted by aid received under the Marshall Plan and the Whitaker–Lemass reforms in the 1950s led to significant growth in the urban population of Dublin in particular.

As a result of the slum clearance programmes of the 1930s and 1940s, there had already been population movements out of the inner city to the north and west of the city, but economic growth in the 1960s led to a rapid expansion in the suburbs ringing the older city lying between the canals. The country was changing, the economy was changing, the city was changing, but the literary iconography of the country was largely unchanging. There were isolated attempts to give voice to an urban experience in the novels of Brian Cleeve, Paul Smith, Lee Dunne and James Plunkett, but these novels either dealt with the traditional inner-city tenement or confined themselves to the stomping grounds of the Dublin professional middle classes. The young, growing population of the suburbs was to find itself without any voice or representation in the various forms of literary expression in the country. The situation would begin to change in the late 1970s with the establishment of the Raven Arts Press and the emergence of writers such as Dermot Bolger and Michael O'Loughlin associated with the press. Their express aim was to provide a means of and a forum for expression for writers growing up in the new and recently established suburbs of Dublin. This was a Dublin which had no place in the rural arcadia of traditionalist representations of the island, but neither did it sit easily with the miserabilist intimacies of the inner city slum.

The problem was not simply one of the objects of representation (suburban versus urban versus rural), it was also to do with the forms of representation. In other words, the Dublin that was emerging in the suburbs to the north and west and south of the city was not only a territory with no trace in the written literature of the country but it was a place that was being profoundly shaped by the sounds and images of modernity. Trying to account for lived experience in this new urban space meant taking on the three-dimensionality (words/music/(moving) pictures) of late twentieth-century suburban Ireland. The mid- to late 1970s sees the emergence of an indigenous music scene in Ireland which would be markedly different from the showband scene which preceded it, but it was a scene which presupposed an already extensive music literacy among both the producers and consumers of popular music in Ireland.[5] The establishment of a national radio and television service in 1961 and the arrival of cable television in Irish cities in the 1970s meant a ready immersion in the popular televisual culture of not only indigenous productions but of television programmes from the United Kingdom and the United States.[6] When the continued popularity of cinema-going as a social practice is taken into account, then it is clear that the culture which comes out of the suburbs will be profoundly diverse in its sources of influence and forms of representation. It is the city which acts as the crucible for the emergence of popular culture in terms of cultural infrastructure (cinemas, music venues, cable television, etc.) and population density, but the representation of the city itself is highly mediated by the forms of popular culture made possible by its existence. In this respect, the novel/film of the Barrytown Trilogy can be seen in its totality as an ambitious attempt to bring together different modes of representation to capture the hybrid complexity of the new urban spaces in Ireland so that, in the words of Martin McLoone, '[t]he most consistent vision of urban Ireland has been in the adaptations of Roddy Doyle's work'.[7]

There are suburbs, of course, and there are suburbs. As much as the different districts of the classic city, the suburbs are subject to the spatial geography of class and the coded class-speak of the postal code. When Doyle claims that 'I would see the first three books anyway as some sort of reflection of working-class life', he is concerned with giving expression to the suburban experience of a specific social class.[8] Part of the experience of the Irish working class has been the 'economic marginalisation' that Lance Pettitt, for example, sees as the driving force behind *The Commitments*.[9] That marginalisation needs to be understood in the particular context of the arrested modernisation that was the lot of the Republic of Ireland in the 1980s. The economic reforms of the 1960s and the tentative moves towards liberalisation of the society in the 1970s would fall foul of two separate developments in the 1980s. The first was the virtual collapse of the economy in the 1980s, with record levels of unemployment, high inflation and substantial net outward migration.[10] The second was the backlash against moves to liberalise social legislation with the 1983 and 1986 abortion and divorce referenda. The triumphant trajectory of modernisation appeared to have been brutally interrupted and once again poverty, joblessness and emigration seemed to be the inevitable fate of the Irish urban poor. Elements of bitterness, hopelessness and the cult of the triumph of failure certainly feature in the Trilogy, both on the printed page and on the screen. However, there is a sense in which Doyle's work and that of the filmmakers Alan Parker and Stephen Frears avoid the facile sentiment of dirty realism in ways that have never failed to incense their critics. We will see in detail how this operates in the case of each novel/film, but for the present it is important to situate Doyle's approach to his material within a general political reading of authenticity.

Doyle himself has noted that, '[i]f you say that you have to be wracked with angst and that you have to write of your direct experience which essentially must be miserable, you're denying an awful lot of people and an awful lot of possibilities'.[11] This is not simply a riposte to the recurrent cliché of the Romantic Artist coughing up bloodstained verse in the garrets of bohemian poverty but it is also directed against those who believe that only certain kinds of writing are politically appropriate to situations of economic and political dispossession. Tragedy and documentary realism are therefore to be the preferred mode for describing the lives and condition of those excluded from the social or economic privileges of a given society. To write or represent otherwise is to become complicit in the sufferings of others, to prefer the easy laugh to the brandished fist. If it is possible to see why politically informed critics can object to the conventional representation of lowlife characters as amiable clowns, it is equally necessary to avoid the tyranny of a kind of pedagogic earnestness which becomes a veiled form of class condescension in its insistence on viewing working-class life in one way and one way only. In answer to the charge that Doyle's characters appear to be devoid of anger about the economic and social condition in which they find themselves, Doyle argues: '"You can't graft anger onto characters just because it suits certain reviewers," he avers. "The reader can make his or her mind up about the characters and what happens to them. The reader doesn't need me to tell him or her how to think."'[12]

The aversion to didacticism which underlies Doyle's position and the aesthetic choices of the two filmmakers is its own response to right-wing censoriousness (moral outrage at bad language, unmarried mothers, etc.) and left-wing indignation (how dare workers laugh at their own plight). Johnny Gogan, in a stinging review of Stephen Frears' film version of *The Snapper* for *Film Ireland*, lambastes the film for its depiction of the locals of Barrytown as 'beer gulping, foul-mouthed, intolerant, inhuman, but all the same happy in their degraded lives. Where have we heard this before? No wonder the middle-class press has been lauding the film. This is a view that the middle class are keen to have of the working class because it is reassuring and unthreatening. To applaud this view is patronising.'[13] Quite apart from the sniffy prudishness of the reviewer's language itself, 'beer gulping, foul-mouthed, intolerant', one could argue that it is equally patronising and as distinctively middle class to have a view of the working class as living lives of unrelieved desperation where humour, shared cultural practices and coping strategies are seen solely as forms of complicity in their own domination. What is threatening and not particularly reassuring about the Barrytown Trilogy on page and on the screen is that it refuses to accept the stock images of the poor as either happy with their lot (as we shall see in the analysis of the films, this is not the case) or morbidly unhappy in a grim re-enactment of an élitist script of class warfare. There is an attempt to view lives from within rather than to judge them from without. And it is a form of viewing that mobilises all the resources that popular culture makes available to the community that is to be expressed as opposed to being labelled.

One resource that attracts attention from the outset is language itself. In the promotional material for *The Commitments*, one of the slogans that was repeatedly used was: '*The Commitments*. At last a film with bollix, tossers, sex, soul, boxes, gooters, the works.' 'Tossers', 'gooters' and the 'works' are among the words explained in 'A Tosser's Glossary', which was distributed with the press pack for *The Commitments*. In a prefatory note to the 'Glossary', Alan Parker offers his own version of Irish linguistic distinctiveness: 'For centuries the Irish were forced to speak English. They got their own back by using it better. From Wilde to Shaw and Beckett to Behan. But the truth is, that the Irish haven't been using English for years. They have their own language. And it isn't Gaelic.'[14] Thus, language itself becomes central to both the promotion of the film and the framing of the cultural distinctiveness of the film. It is noteworthy that Parker, a filmmaker, situates the language in a literary lineage, from 'Wilde to Shaw and Beckett to Behan'. He makes his own the thesis of the Irish Literary Renaissance that, after Douglas Hyde's vernacular translations of Irish poetry, it was possible to create a distinctive Irish culture in the English language.[15] He also, wittingly or unwittingly, articulates the postcolonial reading of language shift in Ireland as formulated by Declan Kiberd, among others, that what the Irish did was to turn linguistic subjection to their own advantage.[16] In what might be termed the Caliban moment in Irish history, the Irish learned the language of the master and then proceeded not simply to curse him but to undo his rule with the words they had been taught.

The situation in the case of the film versions of the Barrytown Trilogy is, however, more complicated and even more subversive than Parker's thumbnail sketch of Irish history would suggest. In the first instance, Parker cites literary precedents for the use of a particular kind of language by the Irish, but the most striking aspect of the film versions of the Barrytown Trilogy is that it would be the first time ever that a whole array of words and Dublin working-class colloquial register would be heard in such a sustained and systematic fashion on the screen. If suburban, working-class Dublin had rarely been seen in the cinema, then it is true to say that it had never been *heard* on screen, literally rendered speechless by the prudishness of producers who worried about how much 'bad' language their audiences could take. Therefore, in analysing the particular soundscape of the film versions of the Trilogy, attention needs to be directed not only to the integration of popular music into the viewer's experience but also to the manner in which the language itself, both as words and as accent (operating at lexical, syntactic and phonetic levels), works to make the films a radical departure in the filmic representation of social class in Ireland.

Timothy Taylor in an article on *The Commitments* is unpersuaded by Parker's linguistic radicalism. He objects to what he sees as the airbrushing of language difference out of the film:

> The film sanitises the novel in the use of a more international English language, for like most films, it was made for mass consumption. Words like 'culchie' from the Irish language wouldn't be understood by non-Irish audiences. So Dublin slang is virtually absent from the film; the only slang we do hear is that which is common to both the United Kingdom and Ireland, words like 'bollix', 'arse' and 'shite'. But the local flavour is gone. The pungency of Dublin English, the use of words from the Irish language, which the English colonizers nearly obliterated, is gone.[17]

The comment, apart from the facile generalisations ('like most films, it was made for mass consumption') and dubious linguistic knowledge ('culchie' is generally believed to be a deformed pronunciation of a place name in County Mayo and not a word from Irish), betrays a specific version of linguistic particularism which is deeply coercive in its implications. Taylor's objection that in the end the audiences of Alan Parker's *The Commitments* are left with a film by an English director about 'semi-exotic musicians who are English – sort of'[18] is an unnerving echo of the worst excesses of irredentism, with its suspicions about the genuine 'Irishness' of the Irish city and town. What is true of the film is also true of the novel, that is, a great deal of the language is in fact shared by the United Kingdom and Ireland, though in many instances words do not have the same frequency of usage nor are they always used in the same context and there are features which are specific to the syntax of Hiberno-English.[19] The implication that this area of commonality is somehow to be decried, that British directors making films about Irish novels where there are similarities in forms of linguistic and cultural expression are by definition engaged in an act of cultural imperialism is poor cultural criticism and worse politics. Parker and Frears, in many respects, are a lot more culturally honest and politically courageous in suggesting the similarities with British working-class culture, which have often been played down because they do not fit into comfortable nationalist narratives about Ireland and its cities.

Forever an affront to the standard-bearers of cultural purism, the mixed origins of cities mean that it would indeed be remarkable, in view of Irish urban history and the story of emigration to Britain, if there were not considerable overlap between cultural practices in urban Ireland and Britain. A much more insidious form of exoticism would in fact have resulted from a relentless attempt to emphasise cultural distinctness and 'pungency', with the attendant dangers of rare-auld-timesism and paddywhackery. In addition, as stated earlier, the considerable influence of popular culture from both Britain and the United States, particularly as mediated through cinema and television, makes the notion of some uncontaminated island of Dublin indigenous culture a misguided fiction.

Nervousness about the particular also has ramifications for the sense of place in the Barrytown Trilogy. What kind of place do Parker and Frears put on the screen and how does this relate to Doyle's own notions of what makes Barrytown a coherent fictional construct? How does place, which has loomed so large in the history of the island, and in cinematographic representations of the island, fare in the Barrytown Trilogy? Again, the succeeding chapters will examine each film in detail, but for the present argument it is useful to outline a general philosophy of place which informs both the novels and film versions. Writing on the film versions of the Barrytown Trilogy, Fintan O'Toole notes that, in the films themselves, 'places are unremarkable, indistinguishable from familiar suburbs around the world'.[20] He goes on to recount a conversation he had with Roddy Doyle while walking around the north Dublin suburb of Kilbarrack, on which Barrytown is loosely based. Doyle points to the buildings and shops around them saying they could be anywhere in Europe and, at one level, this is indeed terrible, because everywhere is just the same. On the other hand, he argues, 'you can look at it and say, "This is great, it's the same as everywhere else", and anyone in Europe is going to understand what you are talking about if you talk about this place. Precisely because it has no real history and very little local colour, it can be an image that most people in the world have access to.'[21] Even if the supposed physical universality of the Dublin suburb invites a certain scepticism (Sarcelles in France does not look remotely like Kilbarrack in Dublin), the more important argument here is that showing Ireland on screen does not inevitably entail picturing Ireland as different. In other words, telling the story of Barrytown to cinema and television audiences does not mean that cinema should take up where the novels left off and provide the establishment shots of recognisably Irish detail to domestic and foreign audiences (though this rule, as we shall see in later chapters, is not universally observed). As non-Irish directors, Parker and Frears did Irish domestic audiences the signal service of by and large disregarding the burden of visual exoticism and allowing them to watch themselves on screen outside the parameters of the picture postcard from elsewhere.

For foreign audiences, part of Doyle's project – and he had a very direct input to the screenplays of two of the films, *The Snapper* and *The Van* – was that place should be made a means of access, not a form of exclusion. In remaining faithful to the specific detail of the suburban locations and resisting the temptation in most instances to somehow frame them as particularly 'Dublin' or 'Irish', both the writer and the filmmakers present working-class Dublin in its genuine specificity (this is how it is) and its accessible universality (this is the kind of place that exists in many contemporary societies). Thus, even if universalist pretensions must always come with a necessary health warning in late modernity, the treatment of place in the films of Parker and Frears points to a way of rehabilitating the supposed 'non-place' or 'empty space' of the suburbs in a place-saturated discourse of national distinctness. They express the complexity of disregarded places, places that are not immediately cinegenic or telegenic in a received visual discourse on Ireland, but in a way that does not fetishise distinctness, that uses particular contexts as a point of departure rather than a port of arrival. What the films of the Barrytown Trilogy signal is the end to a form of Irish exceptionalism. If Ireland from the 1960s onwards sought an experience of modernisation that would in a sense make it not especially different from other countries pursuing the same goal, then there had to be a place in that urban, modernising medium *par excellence*, cinema, for the experiences of these modernised others and the spaces they inhabited, both physical and virtual. The real difference now in Ireland was in not being different.

The band never takes off and the van ends up being driven into the sea. Do Doyle, Parker and Frears then simply add their more contemporary names to the roll-call of triumphant failure in Irish culture? Are they complicit in what Timothy Taylor calls 'the aestheticisation and fetishisation of failure'?[22] Are the films more documentary than actual, snapshots of a beleaguered country in a period of economic depression, useful as social history but condemned by the circumstances of their origin and made redundant by the subsequent fortunes of the Republic? One of the ironies of the move of Ireland into film in the case of the Barrytown Trilogy is that the economic fortunes of the city it is describing are changing dramatically as the films themselves are being made. Between 1987, when *The Commitments* first appears as a novel, and 1996, when *The Van* is shown on the screen for the first time, the economy has been transformed, divorce is about to be legalised, the Provisional IRA has called for one ceasefire and a year later will finally lay down its arms. This did not mean that urban deprivation had gone away, quite the contrary, or that the world of the working-class suburban Barrytowns had been conjured out of existence by the statistical pabulum of the stockbroker economist,[23] but it did mean that the contexts for responding to the work were changing and have changed. Though the seeming hopelessness of the enterprises that are portrayed in *The Commitments* and *The Van* would on the face of it appear to dovetail with a pre-Celtic Tiger ideology of failure, it is important to remember that the one successful undertaking in the Trilogy is birth itself, when Sharon becomes the mother of a child, albeit in less than ideal circumstances. Seeing the trilogy as a whole, indeed as a moment of genesis rather than as a dead-end fetishisation of failure, allows us to re-situate the history of these films in a larger narrative of Irish culture in late modernity.

It is a truism about Irish economic and social life that, with the exception of the north-east, the country moved from the pre-modern to the post-modern and generally missed out on the period of heavy industrialisation that characterised many other European economies and which brought particular forms of modernisation in its wake.[24] Though this thesis can be overstated, there is no doubt that, when Ireland became an integral part of the global economy, the nature of economic activity in developed countries had changed. This crucial shift is what has been referred to as the dematerialisation of production in the developed world. This is the notion that, whereas in the previous industrial mode of production economic benefit was derived from the mass production of material goods (such as cars, fridges, washing machines, etc.), in the informational or post-industrial economy economic gains would accrue from the production of informational or cognitive and postmodern or aesthetic goods.[25] Informational goods are those goods where a premium is placed on the information content. Purchasers of software pay high prices not because of the monetary worth of the material support (the actual disk) but because of the value of the information-processing capability contained in the software. Aesthetic goods are those goods where value resides in the aesthetic component. Buyers of CDs, cinema goers, clients of advertising firms, customers of designer clothes shops, are paying out not for the actual material cost of producing the object they consume but for the added value of the design or aesthetic component. Increasingly, then, the distinction between the cultural industries and the rest of industry becomes a markedly tenuous one.

The power of image as exemplified by the exponential growth of the advertising industry in the late twentieth century is of course closely allied to the growing importance of aesthetic goods in the social and economic lives of developed societies, as is the widespread presence of popular music. In addition, in the case of Ireland and many other developed and developing countries, a crucial economic activity over the years has been tourism, which has relied heavily on the aestheticisation of service delivery and the promotion of the country itself as a particularly desirable aesthetic good. Indeed, one of the constants of Irish cinema and its development has been the necessity to negotiate a viable relationship with the commercial pressures of the tourism picturesque.[26] In the light of these developments, it is possible to view the films in the Barrytown Trilogy as part of a project of generation, as a crucible of change, as the forming of a template for a new kind of Ireland rather than the last chapters in a romance of loss penned by the disaffected. In a context of striking material poverty, the resources that the characters in the films are drawing on are primarily non-material or cultural – music, language, narrative, sport, the intertexts of film and television. Whether the project is forming a band or launching into fast food, the outcomes are closely linked to cultural image, whether it be the street credibility of soul music or the international success of the Irish soccer team. The very fact that all three of the Barrytown novels should be made into films is itself a sign of the new economy of signs, where the image or the aesthetic is central to the way in which the society is evolving. The global success of U2 or *Riverdance* has often been taken to be a symbol of the changing fortunes of the Republic, but to some extent this is to confuse symptom with cause. It is precisely the engagement of the cultural with the economic and the aesthetic with the commercial that allows for the integration of the Republic into the post-industrial economy, not as an afterthought but as a precondition. Two of the three films are, after all, concerned with business and success or failure in business. The films are not about staying quaint and staying put but about staying put and seeing what can be done with the quaint.

It is in view of the tentative emergence of a new form of society and economic activity that it is useful to return to the question of place. As we noted earlier, there is a dual movement towards the specification and universalisation of place in the films. This movement shadows contemporary debates around the notion of glocalisation and the particular relations that exist or might exist between the local and the global.[27] Taking a series of films that were made by non-Irish directors, largely financed by foreign capital and which enjoy considerable success in foreign cinemas or on foreign television screens, notions of identity are bound to be complex. One approach is to view Ireland elsewhere not so much in terms of diasporic identity but from the standpoint of nomadic identity. By this we mean that for Ireland, to travel does not necessarily entail an emigrant culture of displacement with Irishness staked out in specific, historical locales outside of the island. In James Clifford's terms, the Barrytown community is exemplary in travelling-in-dwelling as opposed to dwelling-in-travelling (nobody much travels anywhere in the trilogy, even if *The Van* at some moments has elements of a road movie).[28] This is not only because their language and stories and iconic references constantly point outwards to music, films, sitcoms, crime serials from elsewhere but also because the place in which they dwell now travels courtesy of the director's camera and the distributor's reach.

These are locals being watched by globals and, in a sense, it is the precise nature of their locality which allows them to travel globally to other localities. The nomadic identity of the culture is not to do with rootlessness but with a specific kind of rootedness. The characters belong very definitely to a place, a north Dublin working-class suburb, but it is a place that is and can also be many other places. What the Barrytown Trilogy offers is a way of thinking about culture and identity in cinema which is hostage neither to irredentist particularism nor to abstract universalism. Jan Patočká, in his discussion of the situation of another small nation state in Europe, the Czech Republic, argues that it is perfectly legitimate for a country to wish to develop or elaborate a specific national culture.[29] The difficulty comes from what it decides to do with that culture. In other words, it is the teleological choices of a culture that will define it as oppressive or liberatory. For Patočká, paradoxically, it is the moment when a culture comes into being as distinctive that it should engage in a process of renunciation. In other words, the Czechs should not have a national culture so that it can simply be juxtaposed onto all the other national cultures in Europe but that Czech culture, in its own way, would take part in the movement in Europe which would see each culture renounce its particularist hegemony to express what are the universalist elements in that culture. Thus, the choice does not have to be between particularism and universalism but between two radically different teleologies, one that would seek to impose the particular as the universal and the other which in renouncing the hegemonic pretensions of the particular ensures the continuing value of the particular in reaching out to cultures and places beyond its point of origin. A later commentator on Patočká, Marc Crépon, articulates the argument in the following manner:

> Freedom in effect is not in the withdrawal which restricts individuals to the narrow horizon of their culture – culture in the sense that it belongs to them and protects them behind the borders of their own culture. Culture is synonymous with freedom, from the moment when it can go beyond its own borders by becoming through translation, mediation and exchange, the culture of all – and conversely the culture of others becoming mine, ceases to be the exclusive property of others.[30]

In putting Barrytown on screen, not only is there a long overdue act of cinematographic recognition of the culture elaborated in the working-class suburbs of Dublin, but the Trilogy is also a signal affirmation of a cultural freedom that is an invitation to openness rather than exclusion.

2

THE COMMITMENTS (1991)

When Dave from Eejit Records turns up at a Commitments concert, one of his first comments in the novel is, 'very visual'.[31] It was language rather than visuals, however, which first attracted Alan Parker to *The Commitments*. On reading *The Commitments*, Parker noted that 'It was all dialogue. Very little description. But by using this language and almost nothing but language, in a few lines he made his characters as vivid and as strong as a dozen pages of purple Joycian [*sic*] prose.'[32] The dialogue then would lend it itself to the transition to script, but what about the 'visuals'? How would a form of writing that eschewed descriptive prose make the journey to screen? How would the imagined world of Barrytown, which had few filmic precedents, translate into the cinematographic idiom of a director who had been associated with a number of large, Hollywood-style productions?

Alan Parker, who was born in Islington, north London, in 1944, identifies his north London working-class background with the north Dublin working-class background of Roddy Doyle's novel and claims that a sense of affinity guided him in his work on the film.[33] Parker, who has been knighted for his work, has directed major productions such as *Midnight Express* (1978) and *Evita* (1996) and before embarking on *The Commitments* had long had an interest in music in cinema, from *Bugsy Malone* (1976) to *Fame* (1980) and the Pink Floyd film, *The Wall* (1982).[34] Advertising was a formative experience for Parker and with David Marshall in the early 1970s he ran a very successful company, which produced commercials at the rate of one a week.[35] For an English director to put Ireland on screen in the context of continuing political tensions and violence was not going to be seen as a wholly innocent or neutral engagement, even allowing for Parker's sense of class identification. Lance Pettitt, for his part, sees the involvement of Parker in the context of the benighted state of the Irish film industry of the period: 'In the absence of both the [Irish] Film Board and significant funding from RTÉ, it was almost inevitable that Anglo-American film interests would move into the gap to support (and profit from) Irish-themed films.'[36] It is noteworthy that Parker himself defended his desire to make a film such as *The Commitments* on the grounds that he wanted to break the monopoly of Troubles-centred representations of Ireland on screen: 'It's not about the problem of the six counties of the north. There is life in Ireland other than the conflict.'[37] The difficulty, of course, is that politics do not stop at borders and that conflict can take many forms, whether it be tension between social classes, competing versions of gender or the way in which a community is presented to the larger world. The 'visuals' tell their own story about how conflicts are articulated and they represent so many commitments to versions of a social or political truth.

In the novel, when Jimmy Rabbitte Jr gathers together his group he has an explicit political agenda for them. Soul in Rabbitte's view is about two things, sex and politics, and this makes it refreshingly and usefully different from other forms of music. However, the politics is a politics of disenchantment with the established political parties – 'Not songs abou' Fianna fuckin' Fáil or annythin' like tha'' – and more a politics of location. So he announces to a stunned Outspan and Derek, other members of the proposed group:

> —The Irish are the niggers of Europe, lads.
>
> They nearly gasped: it was so true.
>
> —An' Dubliners are the niggers of Ireland. The culchies have fuckin' everythin'. An' the northside Dubliners are the niggers o' Dublin.
>
> —Say it loud, I'm black an' I'm proud.[38]

In the film, the scene is transposed to a video shop, the racially offensive 'niggers' is replaced by 'blacks' and there is no mention of the 'culchies' having everything. If Derek and Outspan are stunned in the novel, they and the other members of the group, as Timothy Taylor has pointed out, look more incredulous than impressed in the film.[39] In a later scene shot on the DART, Jimmy (Robert Arkins) speaks of soul as the 'rhythm o' the factory. The workin' man's rhythm' – only to be told by Natalie (Maria Doyle) that there's not 'much rhythm in guttin' fish'. In the novel, Jimmy goes on to lambaste Irish party politics, claiming that neither the Left (Labour Party, the Workers' Party) nor the Right (Fianna Fáil) have any 'soul', but these specific Irish political references are absent from the film. The repeated looks of bewilderment on the faces of the other band members in the film to Jimmy's brief political interventions can be seen as another form of hostility to a leaden didacticism which risks being counter-productive, as indicated in the introduction to this study. However, more interesting from the point of view of the film itself is the way in which a politics of location is worked out. The film elides political detail, in that the anger of the book directed at the perceived bankruptcy of Irish party politics is absent from the film. But if the film was to be shown to audiences outside Ireland (which it was, very successfully, except for the US), then what would they make of references to largely unknown political parties from a small island off the west coast of Europe? On the other hand, without those references, does the political resonance to the music make any sense?

The answer to these questions partly lies in the very choice of music by the Commitments. In choosing soul music, the film does make it clear that the music is seen as the music of the African-American working class and that Jimmy regards the music as answering to the political and economic marginalisation of himself and his working-class friends. In doing this, of course, he is transporting soul music from its specific American context to an Irish or Dublin situation and unmooring it from its own cluster of local detail. The music, in speaking of particular forms of dispossession, is also a music that can speak to other people in other times and in other places. Similarly, Jimmy's claim that 'I'm black an' I'm proud', which can appear to be an egregious appropriation of hardship suffered by others, does need to be set in the context of a rights discourse that can and did travel from Alabama to Antrim.[40] In order for the particular to have a more general currency, it is necessary to suggest or hint at a framework for identification.

Parker interpolates a scene in *The Commitments* (which is not in the novel) where Jimmy goes to the hatch in the unemployment exchange in Werburgh Street and is reprimanded by the clerk for not having found a job in two years. His immediate response is to ask her whether she knew or not that Ireland was a 'third world country'. The decade in which the novel was written was one of severe economic deprivation and high unemployment and many analysts looking at the fortunes of Irish society and the economy since independence interpreted it as being that of a third-world country mired in the contradictions of the post-colonial.[41] The film has Jimmy unemployed, whereas he is employed in the novel, and he has to use contacts with violent petty criminals to get sound equipment, again a story element which is present in the film but absent from the novel. Jimmy's circumstances then are more desperate in the film than in the novel, and from selling bootleg videos to dealing with the criminal underworld, the society in which he moves on screen is even more marginalised than the one in the pages of the novel. The difficulty is how does this 'third world country' escape the deprivation tourism of directors for whom, as Fintan O'Toole has pointed out, one people's realism becomes another's exotica.[42]

In the long opening sequence of the film where the camera follows Jimmy through a street market trying to sell his goods, the market could be in another century (Plate 1). The very first shot is of horses being sold and an early shot is of a ballad singer belting out the 'Springhill Mining Disaster', unaccompanied, as if he were giving voice to a comeallye at a horse fair in nineteenth-century Ireland. The crowds, the bustling market scene, the older forms of transportation

Plate 1. Jimmy at the market

(horses), do fit into a conventional representation on screen of the developing world and these opening shots clearly situate Jimmy in what is, to all intents and purposes, a 'third world' context. This is in many ways an Ireland that is instantly recognisable as a land of poverty, song and picturesque anachronisms. These are the establishment shots not of sublime emptiness but of Dickensian fullness, of a bustling neighbourhood of riotous proximity. In his description of location hunting with the Production Designer, Brian Morris, Parker claimed that it was 'our intention at all times to avoid the picture postcard locales traditionally associated with Ireland and show a contemporary world a little different from the romantic notions normally associated with films about Ireland'. In order to do this, Parker and Morris 'put together a patchwork of places, streets, buildings of a world we could see but could not find in one place', aiming at striking 'a balance between the bland 50s boredom of the Northside housing estates and the older city centre'.[43] So scenes are shot for example in Smithfield in the north inner city, Ballymun in the northside suburbs and Sir John Rogerson Quay in the south inner city, to name but a view of the locations. The composite nature of the city is vaguely reminiscent of films about Ireland from the silent era, where the dramatic action would switch between different beauty spots in the country to enhance recognition and appeal to the vulgate of the sublime. Then, we had a composite Ireland, now we have a composite Dublin. There is a further irony in that it is precisely out of the 'bland 50s boredom of the Northside housing estates' that the writing of Doyle and the Commitments themselves emerge. And when Doyle becomes sole author of the screenplay, as he does with *The Snapper* and *The Van*, the action is firmly situated in the world of the 'Northside housing estates', namely Kilbarrack.

Brian Guckian in his review of *The Commitments* argues that the film is none the less 'an honest portrayal of Dublin and her people, and all the more welcome for that'. This is because, in part, 'Gale Tattersall's photography (rainy streets, drab housing, smoky halls) never lets us lose sight of reality'.[44] It is from the perspective of a desire to convey a particular kind of reality that it is possible to locate the multiple locations of the film. In other words, if place politics rather than party politics count then the film must in a sense politicise rather than neutralise place. That sense of place, however, is much more obviously a matter of class and of circumstances than of geography. If Dubliners are the 'blacks' of Ireland and northside Dubliners are the 'blacks' of Dublin, the statement can only make sense in terms of the experience of *specific* kinds of Dubliners who are united by social exclusion. The statement can no more apply to the comfortable sections of the north Dublin bourgeoisie than it can exclude the working-class populations in the south inner city or working-class suburbs to the south-west of the city. In this respect, the locational promiscuity of the film is truer to the core political message of Jimmy Rabbitte's declarations in that it unites on the screen, in a synthetic representation of the city, the disparate centres of poverty and marginalisation. Like the very act of fiction itself, the camera has to lie to tell the truth. The world of deprivation is one that, in order to be 'seen', cannot be shown as simply existing 'in one place', although the 'one place' that does feature on the screen is Dublin itself.

As we mentioned earlier, the translatability of soul to an Irish urban context is evidence of the open-endedness of the music itself, which allows it to be performed and absorbed in other environments and circumstances. The ambition of Jimmy Rabbitte is not only that a future band play soul music, but that they play 'Dublin soul'. But what is Dublin soul? At one point in the novel, the narrator declares 'Dublin soul was about to be born'. The Commitments are playing their first concert in the community centre and they have been giving a rendition of 'Night Train' when Deco alters the lyrics:

> Deco growled: —STARTIN' OFF IN CONNOLLY—
> The train in the hall stopped as they waited to hear what was going to follow that.
> Deco was travelling north, by D.A.R.T.
> —MOVIN' ON OU' TO KILLESTER—
> They laughed. This was great. They pushed up to the stage.
> —HARMONSTOWN RAHENY—
> They cheered.
> —AN' DON'T FORGET KILBARRACK – THE HOME O' THE BLUES—
> Dublin soul had been delivered.[45]

Other modifications of lyrics in soul songs bring in references to pints of Guinness and meeting under Clery's clock. So Dublin soul in the novel is essentially a matter of words, of localising the references so that they take on added meaning and resonance for the audiences. In the film, of course, there are no such modifications of lyrics and the Commitments, rather like the wedding band we are introduced to early on in the film, are content to play cover versions of songs with no local Dublin or Irish references. Does this mean then that the band could be any band anywhere, lost in a delirium of derivation? When Alan Parker says 'Our film is set in Dublin, Ireland but it's about the hopes and dreams music brings to young kids everywhere, from Finglas to Philadelphia and Memphis to Minsk',[46] is there a sense that the young kids from everywhere end up playing music that is nowhere?

The more pessimistic answers to these questions are contradicted by the musical dynamic of the film itself, where local reference and specific context in musical terms are a matter more for the soundtrack than for the lyric sheets. When Jimmy puts an advertisement in the paper looking for musicians with the caveat that 'rednecks and southsiders need not apply', the film presents us with a long, tightly edited sequence of images showing a plethora of musical hopefuls. These include a heavy metal singer (Jezz Bell) singing 'Blood! Blood! Blood!', a fiddle auditioner (Colm Mac an Iomaire), a punk girl singer (Emily Dawson), an uileann pipe player (Brian Mac Aodha), a Cajun trio (Patrick Foy/Alan Murray/Jody Campbell), a young woman singing a Smiths song, 'Heaven Knows I'm Miserable Now' (Canice William), another young woman singing 'I Dreamed a Dream' from *Les Misérables* (Tricia Smith) and the three-member Coconuts Trio singing 'Poppa Joe' (Dave Kane/Kristel Harris/Maria Place). The question that Jimmy puts to all potential band hopefuls is what are their 'influences'. The film's response is that they are multiple and various. The auditions do not feature prominently in the novel and the range of influences cited are relatively restricted (U2/Simple Minds/Led Zeppelin/Jethro Tull/Bachman Turner Overdrive). In the film, what is striking is that the musical backdrop for the Commitments includes everything from indigenous folk music to world music to heavy metal and punk and international popular music. In other words, the band emerges from a musical context that sees the indigenous and imported, the popular and the progressive, the experimental and the esoteric, all co-exist alongside each other. The distinctness of the environment in which the Commitments create their music on screen lies not in its exclusiveness but in its relatedness. What constitutes the specificity of the musical culture is the co-existence and blend of different influences, the way in which the singers and musicians relate to music from many different places, on both a local and a global scale. Rather than a notion of the city or indeed the country being the unpolluted reservoir of indigenous musical purity, *The Commitments* in the long auditioning sequence portrays the culture's specific strengths as lying in its porousness. The Commitments, in turn, by performing the kind of music they perform, contribute to the relational richness of an Irish musical culture which of course had come to international prominence in the 1980s.

The auditions were not only on the set but off it, in that Parker set up auditions to find singers and musicians for the band in the film. In June 1990 he arrived in Dublin and immediately 'began the auditions process, listening to 64 bands at ten minute intervals playing everything from heavy metal to hip hop and folk to funk'. Parker decided to cast the net as widely as possible and organised 'an open casting call at the Mansion House (town hall) where we invited anyone in Dublin who wanted to be considered for the film. Over 1500 young hopefuls turned up reading a page of the script and singing and playing everything from guitars to tin whistles, banjos to bagpipes.' Parker's aim was that the making of the film itself would parallel the making of the band: 'In the book and the film the band members take their first steps hesitantly, being downright awful in their early rehearsals, but gradually improve culminating in their brief success at the end of our story.'[47] Parker's desire for a mimetic authenticity has not always met with favourable comment. Fintan O'Toole, for example, argues that the choice of a largely amateur cast is based on a mistaken notion of authenticity. By casting 'real' young people as actors rather than actors, audiences will be given 'not a recreation of Dublin's youth culture but the thing itself'. In his view, Parker is mistaken about the young Dubliners in Doyle's novel in that they are not untutored Irish exotics but musically savvy young adults who are wholly *au fait* with the popular music they aspire to play, in both the musical and dramatic sense of performance. Hence, 'By imposing the idea of authenticity on the story through the casting of nonactors, Parker misses the point.'[48]

It is difficult to see how this criticism can be sustained by the evidence of the film itself, as, irrespective of how the actors were recruited, there is nothing in particular to suggest that they are 'romantic Irish exotics'. Indeed, the most exotic leading character, Joey the Lips Fagan (Johnny Murphy), was the only well-known professional actor in the group. By incorporating the auditions process into the film, Parker makes explicit the musical sophistication of the culture from which the young performers emerge. To this end there are 68 different musical cues in the film, including 52 different songs (21 of these songs are sung by the Commitments proper). There is no sense, then, in which they are noble savages whose cachet lies in their musical benightedness. On the contrary, 'authenticity' is more a matter of process than origins. That is to say, what makes the music 'real' and the performances effective is not that most of the actors happen to be non-professional actors from Ireland but that they encounter all manner of musical and personal difficulties in their attempt to create music together, despite their prior musical knowingness. To the extent that *The Commitments* is a film dealing in a type of realism of process, seeing the choice of 'nonactors' as a misguided realism based on alleged stereotypes of belonging is also in a sense to miss the point. That that process is central to the realisation of the film is borne out by the specific attention to the technical rendition of the music in performance:

> We had decided to use a new system for shooting and recording the music which had never before been used on a film. Most film music from *Singin' in the Rain* to MTV uses pre-recorded tracks and vocals which are played back as the camera takes up different positions with the artists miming. I wanted to capture the reality of the rehearsals and performing by recording the vocals live on set. This is very difficult as modern film requires many different angles to be covered and a constant sound track is needed in order for the finished edited scene to match cut by cut. We used a new system of out-of-phase speakers which enabled us to play the

pre-recorded constant backing tracks at maximum volume to give us live performance atmosphere for the vocalists to sing to. Each vocal was then recorded live onto a twenty-four track recorder that was on set with us. Because of the out-of-phase speakers the vocals could be recorded cleanly for re-mixing later. This allowed us the technical precision needed for a complicated cut but gave us the truth, energy and spirit of a live performance.[49]

In conveying the 'truth, energy and spirit' of the music, we get shots of members of the band performing in particular locations. For example, in one scene we find the three backing singers performing a dance routine in the courtyard of a Dublin Corporation flats complex, with washing lines much in evidence and a miniature statue of the Virgin Mary on view (Plate 2). Other shots are on a Dublin bus or in a meat factory. The musical comedy as a soundtrack performed against a *Sound of Music* set of visual postcards is deliberately eschewed. In the context of the fusion of music and image to sell Ireland as a pre-modern ecological playground to the jaded urban élites of the planet, the studied anti-romanticism of the

Plate 2. Imelda, Bernie and Natalie and the Blessed Virgin

locations chosen to situate action or performance show that the process of reinventing Ireland is not only a musical undertaking but a visual one. At one moment in the film, relaying a scene from the novel, the band lines up for a photograph. When the photographer wonders whether they should include Butt Bridge to make the photograph more attractive, Jimmy is adamant that he does not want the picture postcard backdrop of the city but an image of urban decay (Plate 3). Gale Tattersall as director of photography obliges in the film with repeated shots of dilapidated interiors and exteriors. A recurrent feature of the shots is that the rundown streets and flat complexes are presented as teeming with children, the decaying material infrastructure of the city contrasted with the anarchic energies of the predominantly young population. In addition, if the preferred landscapes of the tourist sublime are the empty vistas of land, sea and sky, the urban scenes in *The Commitments* are generally alive with human subjects and filled with human incident.

The Commitments, under Jimmy, are committed to their own version of a musical truth, but they are also committed to a visual truth about the city in which they grew up. The difficulty, of course, is that one generation's visual truth becomes the next's visual cliché.

Plate 3. Group photograph of The Commitments

Grubby realism and shots of urban ruin harden into cinematographic convention and it is easy to parody the narcissism of misery if the director projects a uniformly bleak urban environment. However, it is also worth remembering the contribution a major production like *The Commitments* can make to the clearing out of visual space, where other images of Ireland and particularly of the city could make their way onto the screen. The ramshackle state of the city is as important a statement of the politics of the Commitments as Jimmy's oracular pronouncements. This is a city whose crumbling and shabby streets, complexes and estates have apparently no economic future to offer to the kids who mill around the container in the yard or play with animals on waste ground. The aural promise of the music then is constantly undercut by the visible decay on the streets. It is of course the relative youth of the population, very clearly and repeatedly signalled in Parker's film, which would later come to be seen as a vital asset in Ireland's economic regeneration at the close of the twentieth century.[50] As with the other films in the Barrytown Trilogy, the capacity for change in the society is signalled, the presence of utopian promise marked, through the determined effort of a Rabbitte or a Curley not to confuse fate (things as they are) with destiny (things as they must be). Neither Parker nor Frears, however, buy into the fiction of a naïve, Thatcherite, self-help voluntarism and the camera tells us as much about the social obstacles that need to be overcome as the pronouncements of a Jimmy Rabbitte or a Sharon or Larry Curley.

In a scene in the novel which makes it onto screen in a truncated form, Joey the Lips Fagan describes his religious conversion to Jimmy and then tells of his decision to return to Ireland. A Baptist minister called Ed Winchell had been watching 'something on TV about the feuding brothers in Northern Ireland and The Lord told the Reverend Ed that the Irish brothers had no soul, that they needed some soul. And pretty fucking quick! Ed told me to go back to Ireland and blow some soul into the Irish Brothers. The Brothers wouldn't be shooting the asses off each other if they had soul.'[51] In the film, Joey repeats the phrase about the Irish brothers 'shooting the asses off each other' when members of the band gather together in the building to the back of his mother's house. Though, as we saw earlier, Parker despaired of Ireland always being associated with political and sectarian conflict on the screen (big and small), Joey the Lips draws politics and religion together in his own particular way. If Joey's conviction is that the Irish brothers need 'soul', how does the film situate itself with respect to religious belief and practice, long held to be one of the defining parameters of identities in Ireland? As a film which Lance Pettitt discusses under the heading of 'Box Office Irish', does *The Commitments* refute or pander to conventional images of the Irish as being particularly or unusually religiose? The film like the novel after all is about 'soul' music, so to what extent are considerations on the Irish soul to the fore in the film or does Parker – like Doyle – deliberately exploit the ambiguity of the word to challenge stereotypical versions of Irish involvement with religious belief and institutional religion? A character who is alluded to in the novel but is represented more fully in the film is Joey the Lips' mother (Maura O'Malley). In one of the first encounters between the band members and Joey's mother the camera picks out a portrait of Pope Paul VI on the wall behind them. In a later scene, Joey's mother is depicted alone, surrounded by religious icons, playing the violin and singing the Marian hymn, 'Star of the Sea', and a strikingly similar scene is presented at the very end of the film when Jimmy details the subsequent career of the band members (Plate 4). In the case of the medical student, Steven Clifford (Michael Aherne), one scene has him playing 'Nights in White Satin' on the organ in the Carmelite church in Whitefriar Street and in another he is shown confessing to sins of blasphemy and lustfulness before having a musical reference corrected by the priest on the other side of the grille.

It is possible to see the interpolation of these scenes which do not figure in the novel as evidence of Hollywoodian bad faith, a kind of

Plate 4. Joey's mother and 'Star of the Sea'

iconic laziness that has religion as a marker of Irishness in the way that bulls become a marker of Spanishness and sexual tease a marker of Frenchness. However, it is important to situate these scenes with respect to the characters involved. Joey Fagan's mother is elderly and has grown up in a markedly different Ireland from that of the young band members of the Commitments (young, that is, with the exception of her son Joey). It is understandable, predictable even, that, in a period of change, she will seek solace in the belief system of her childhood or formative years. In a sense, the film is more sociologically complex than the novel, in showing that no generation has a monopoly on the totality of experiences in a society. The religiosity of Joey's mother both marks a past against which the various forms of Irish modernisation define themselves but it also signals its increasingly peripheral status through the very isolation of the mother in the two scenes where she is shown playing her Marian hymns. A further dimension to religious references in the film is that they are both related to music: Steven playing the organ and Joey's mother on the violin are evidence of a musical strand in the culture which is closely linked to institutional religion. If the close involvement of the Church in the social structures of the society is signalled through having to get permission from the local curate and his committee for the first Commitments concert, the traditional class alignment of the Church is underscored by the fact that it is the middle-class medical student Steven who is presented in the film as the most conspicuously pious. So rather than the foregrounding of religion in these scenes simply being awkward attempts at local colour, they make their own internally sophisticated comments about a society which cannot miraculously disavow its past and its class structure in an act of wishful, amnesiac modernisation.

If Joey's mother embraces a particular notion of the salvation of the soul, what of Joey himself and the other characters in the film? One of the early close-ups we get in the film is of two images placed over each other in the Rabbitte household of Pope John Paul II and Elvis Presley (Plate 5). Jimmy's father (Colm Meaney) has already announced to his son that Elvis is in fact God. When Joey tells of his meeting with Elvis, he is listened to with the utmost reverence by Jimmy Rabbitte Sr, as if he were recounting a divine apparition or an encounter with the sacred. Jimmy Rabbitte Sr's son, Jimmy, is exemplary in his filial piety, not so much in embracing the music of Elvis but in sharing a belief that music is somehow sacred, that the Pope and a Popular Singer do belong on the wall together. Jimmy Rabbitte Jr, if nothing else, curiously resembles a messianic figure, preaching his particular gospel of soul to the members of the band, a fact ironically underscored by the repeated close-ups of the clean-shaven Messiah as he lays down the laws of soul to print journalists and band members. For what Jimmy promises to the performers in the Commitments is remarkably similar to the claims of institutional religions, namely a belief system which makes sense of experience and a transformative or transcendental dimension which lifts believers out of the ordinary on to another plane of existence. When the commitment of the Commitments begins to flag, Jimmy asks them do they want to 'stand out' or simply be like the rest of the 'tossers' around them. Performing music is to be part of an elect who want

Plate 5. The Pope and Elvis

something different and who believe in Jimmy's credo of sexual honesty and class politics. The sense of promise is expressly articulated by Bernie (Bronagh Gallagher) when Jimmy goes to see her in her flat in Ballymun. She has been missing rehearsals and

Jimmy wants to know if she still wants to sing with the band. In one shot she is at the ironing board and behind her is a clearly visible reproduction of a painting showing the Sacred Heart. Her dialogue is interrupted by a crying child and she is clearly under stress from her circumstances. She tells Jimmy that 'she needs something to look forward to' and that the band is more important to her than anyone else in the group. In framing Bernie and the Sacred Heart, there is a certain element of parody as she roundly abuses Jimmy and the child, undercutting any traditional image of a dutiful Martha or a meek Mary revelling in the self-abnegation of sacrifice. However, the juxtaposition of the sacred and the secular also shows that it is through culture in the form of popular music that Bernie wants to change her life, not through a religion which had in Irish society been deeply implicated in the cruel and inhuman treatment of unmarried mothers in religious-run institutions. If Bernie is turning her back on the religious icon, it is partly because the future offered by Jimmy allows her to bring a credible, transformative vision to her straitened circumstances. Whether Jimmy's ill-defined ethics of personal and communal liberation are credible or not is less important than the fact that the film signals a decisive shift in Irish society towards new belief systems, new forms of transcendence and new definitions of what constitute not only Dublin but Irish soul.

One of the new definitions proposed by Jimmy Rabbitte Jr in both the novel and the film has to do with questions of gender. In the novel, Jimmy explains the 'mission' of the Commitments to a journalist from the *Northside News*. Among other things, Jimmy claims: 'We're against racial and sexual discrimination an' heroin.'[52] In the film, the journalist (Phelim Drew) is from the *Evening Herald* and the message is the same. But if, in Jimmy's words, soul music is the 'rhythm of ridin'' and the three female singers are referred to earlier in the film as 'The Commitmentettes', is there a sense in which the women in the film are secondary to the male characters and the sites of explicit male sexual fantasy, captured in the scene where faces of the male band members are pressed to the window watching Imelda Quirke (Angeline Ball) descend a ladder? Roddy Doyle has cited gender as one of his reasons for deciding to write about a soul band in his novel rather than any other kind of band: ' "Most bands are 3 or 4, usually male", he explains. "So I decided a soul band would be far more interesting, insofar as you'd also have a brass section and female backing vocalists, which would make a bigger and more interesting band." '[53] In his comments on the making of *The Commitments*, Alan Parker talked of his own desiderata when it came to casting the female singers for the group. He did not want 'bimbo types' but young women who were 'gutsier' than the stereotypical norm. In a critical evaluation of his own film, he concluded that the young women were as strong if not 'stronger' than the men portrayed on screen.[54] If sexual honesty is at the core of Jimmy's philosophy for the group, then it is sexual tension that comes to be the group's undoing. One element of that tension is to do with Deco Cuffe's (Andrew Strong) role as lead singer and his hostility to Imelda, Natalie and Bernie any time that they are either singing solo or simply without him. When this happens the camera cross-cuts to an unhappy Deco either on or off stage or we have a scene where Deco brutally interrupts Natalie's singing of 'Jimmy Mo Mhíle Stór' with frenzied banging on the drums while waiting for rehearsals to begin. Although it is Jimmy who repeatedly refers to the importance of sex as part of the philosophy of soul, this belief appears to be largely an exercise in rhetoric, as it is Natalie and Imelda walking home from the factory who are frank in their discussion of sexual attraction and who use sexual language as a weapon against the macho condescension of Deco.

The break with the male monsters of the rock genre is clearly indicated in the rehearsal scene where the crying child is foregrounded in the shot of three backing singers (Plate 6). The child is not only a reminder of the reality beyond the enchanted world of the musical but positions women differently in the popular music film

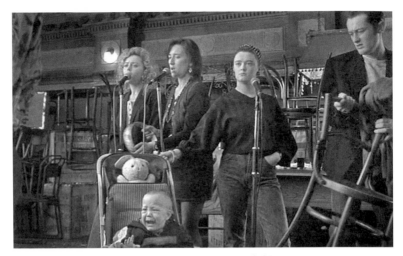

Plate 6. Imelda, Natalie, Bernie and crying child

genre by having a performer, Bernie, who is also a single mother and who does not fit into the mould of the glamorous, unattached if doomed lead singer or the glamorous, unattached but unnoticed backing singer. It is Bernie who is repeatedly sceptical about Jimmy's high-flown language of sexual emancipation and who is suspicious of the sexual motives of the male characters, puncturing easy sentiment or undoing the duplicity of romantic kitsch. If Natalie, Bernie and Imelda perform a dance routine alongside the statue of the Virgin Mary, it is an acknowledgement of the fact that they are no longer content to play the role that was traditionally assigned to them by a patriarchal Church and society. They are no longer the frozen icons of submissive piety but dynamic subjects of processes that they seek to control. In this respect, it is hardly surprising at the end of the film that, when we are presented with the current activities of the members of the band, it is the women who are the most successful, with two out of the three singers performing as lead singers with their own groups. In other words, Jimmy has partly delivered on the mission of soul but not in the way that he or many of the other male members of the band had anticipated. It is the women (with the possible exception of Imelda) whose lives are the most radically transformed by the music-making of the Commitments and who embody the metamorphic potential of the music itself.

Lance Pettitt has observed how *The Commitments* takes on a theme dear to Hollywood narrative, the success story:

> There might seem to be a world of difference between the USA and northside Dublin, but *The Commitments* not only features characters whose everyday lives are imbued with American ideas, but the narrative of the film itself provides a working example of the American dream of success that occupies a central place in Hollywood films.[55]

Timothy Taylor, for his part, bemoans the fact that 'Dublin's problems, arising from Ireland's years as a British colony, take a backseat to concerns for moving the plot along, or, in the case of the film, presenting covers of great songs'.[56] A successful film about an unsuccessful band inevitably invites suspicion about the nature of success in cinematography. In addition, a feeling that an independent Ireland merely made the transition from British colony to American state can be borne out by a reading of the film that sees it as parroting the values of mainstream Hollywood cinema. However, such a reading is to project a notion of success on to the film which is gainsayed by the pronouncements and behaviour of the band members themselves. The music the band play is largely American, but as we saw earlier the film clearly delineates a specifically Irish musical context from which the musicians emerge. In fact, part of the specific achievement of the film is that the band play American soul music and do not feel that physical geography is musical destiny and so feel compelled to play music that is somehow readily identifiable as Irish. It is not so much that the characters are 'imbued with American ideas' (which are, in any case, notoriously difficult to define), but that members of the band are literate in the popular culture of their time, which is predominantly but not exclusively American in origin.

The desire for success is not a validation of on-your-bike liberalism but, on the contrary, an indictment of a political environment and social circumstances which expose much of the shallowness of the entrepreneurial promise. Although it is easy to be cynical about Jimmy's politicisation of the music, which is as puzzling to some of the band members as it is to the journalist from the *Evening Herald* (who has to be reminded to spell 'guerrilla' with a 'u' rather than an 'o'), it nevertheless, like Gale Tattersall's photography, frames the conduct and evolution of the band. The one character, Deco, who most ostensibly embraces the cult of success and stardom is in fact almost universally reviled. The principal difficulty for most of the members of the Commitments is not so much external as internal colonisation. That is to say, the working-class members of the group find that Dublin's problems are not so much to do with being a former British colony as being a contemporary Irish colony, a dependent minority within the structure of the independent state. If Jimmy is adamant that 'Southsiders and rednecks' should not apply to join his band and that 'Northsiders are the blacks of Dublin', he is articulating a clear class geography that complicates what can be the excessively reductionist identity politics of post-colonial analysis.

In the film, as in the other two films in the Barrytown Trilogy, nobody in a position of legitimate authority speaks with a working-class Dublin accent. From the clerk in the unemployment exchange to the priest in the church aisle and the print journalist, anyone who is invested with even a modicum of authority speaks differently. The problem faced by Jimmy and most of his friends is not the occupying force of a foreign army but the hermetic exclusivism of indigenous class privilege and the social apartheid of the city. The hostility in the film to particular forms of music, from 'Art School' to jazz, is firmly located in a profound class resentment. When the band place their first concert under the aegis of the anti-drugs campaign, they find that the word 'heroin' has been misspelt as 'heroine', but this prompts the comment that it does not matter 'because no one around here can spell'. Comic device aside, the rubbed-out 'e' on the banner is eloquent about the complicity of educational and social exclusion in the capital city of a Republic which professes the equality of all its citizens. The Commitments in their coming together are as much about political commitments that have not been honoured as they are about a group of young musicians dreaming of being Stars for a Day or more. The band members do not speculate on the material pay-off of putative success. If a great deal of the film is showing the band either playing music or preparing for it or organising the infrastructure to make it happen, it is because the film is primarily bound up with a politics of collective recognition rather than an economics of self-advancement. *The Commitments* is ultimately not so much to do with the triumph of failure as with the failure of triumphalism. The Commitments are there where the (social and political) commitment is not.

3

THE SNAPPER (1993)

In the shift from *The Commitments* to *The Snapper* we have the move from a film made primarily for a film theatre audience to a film which is made for television broadcast. This shift also parallels a change in director, with Stephen Frears, a veteran of film production for television, directing both *The Snapper* and *The Van*. Doyle declared himself to be on the whole satisfied with the work of Alan Parker on *The Commitments*, but his concerns over artistic control led him to want to be more directly involved in subsequent film versions of his work:

> 'With *The Commitments*, I was very pleased with the end result but it was pure luck,' he explains, 'It could've gone to a director with half the talent, a third of the brain and none of the sensitivity of Alan Parker. It could just as easily have been a monumental disaster and I could've done nothing about it. I could've given back the money I earned and asked that my name be taken off the credits but it would still have been a disaster. And having just luckily escaped with *The Commitments*, I decided that was never going to happen again.'[57]

Doyle insisted on the right to choose the producer for any subsequent films and for the right to pull out and take his book with him if he was not happy with the direction of the film. In addition, he asked that he be sole author of the screenplay. The BBC agreed to all these conditions and Doyle chose Linda Myles as producer, whom he had met on the film set of *The Commitments*. It was Myles who encouraged Stephen Frears to become involved in directing the film.

Frears, who was born in 1941 in Leicester, went on to study law in Cambridge but on leaving university became increasingly involved in film. He joined the Royal Court Theatre in London on a directorial apprenticeship and later went on to work as a directorial assistant in film. He worked with Karl Reisz on *Morgan – A Suitable Case for Treatment* (1966), with Albert Finney on *Charlie Bubbles* (1968) and with Lindsay Anderson on *If...* (1968). His own directorial debut was a short film on racial tension in South Africa called *The Burning* (1967). He is a prolific director and between 1967 and 2002, for example, he directed over 43 films, although only nine films were released as film theatre movies.[58] Though primarily associated with BBC TV Drama, Frears did direct two films in Hollywood, *The Grifters* (1990) and *Accidental Hero* (1992). Before *The Snapper*, Frears had been associated in the preceding decade with films as different as *My Beautiful Laundrette* (1985) and *Dangerous Liaisons* (1988).

Frears is also notable for working closely with writers and has in the past collaborated with writers such as Neville Smith, Tom Stoppard, Christopher Hampton, Peter Prince, Alan Bennett, Hanif Kureishi and David Hare. Therefore, for a writer seeking to work closely with a director, Frears was in many respects an obvious choice. Doyle noted that he was relieved to discover that 'Frears was a modest man'[59] and the theme of modesty is picked up by David Thomson, who argues that films with relatively modest budgets and schedules are in keeping with the modest character of the director. Thomson further adds that Frears' strengths lie in the fact that 'he surely understands the English class system, the varieties of place in Britain, and the various subterfuges that block candor'.[60] It is not always the case that modesty is a virtue with respect to a critical reputation and the danger is that the actual complexity and sophistication of a film such as *The Snapper* could be overlooked. The film's origins in television further add to a certain marginalisation, with a scale of value according higher status to film theatre productions over 'films for television', particularly in view of the precedent set by the filmmaking of Alan Parker.

It is noteworthy that in Brown's assessment of Frears' cinematographic virtues he specifically refers to his familiarity with the English class system and the 'varieties of place in Britain'. If sensitivity to context and local detail are of importance, then what are the implications of this for a director who is dealing with an Irish subject? In a film directed for the British Broadcasting Corporation, to what extent is Ireland going into film or is it Suburban Anywhere going into film, or is the film another variation on stage Irish folk doing hilarious things in their quaintly broken-down lives? An immediate context for the making of the film itself was the debate around the so-called 'X case' in 1992–1993 where a fourteen-year-old girl who had been sexually assaulted and become pregnant was prevented from leaving the country for an abortion by the Attorney General on foot of his interpretation of the 1983 amendment to the Irish Constitution protecting the right to life of the unborn. One outcome, indeed, of the bitter and virulent campaign leading to the passing of the amendment was the censorship of any information on abortion facilities in Britain or elsewhere. In addition, the failure of the divorce referendum in 1986 and the discrediting of Garret Fitzgerald's Constitutional Crusade resulted in sharp divisions in the body politic and civil society at large. Thus, issues around marriage, family, sexuality and pregnancy were to the fore in the fraught ideological and moral climate of the 1980s and early 1990s, with pressure groups such as Family Solidarity seeking to align social legislation with Catholic teaching on moral issues. Making a film set in Ireland in 1993 about an unplanned pregnancy after a sexual assault on a young woman by a married man was to invite readings of the film which could not ignore the social and political realities of Ireland. Indeed, reactions to those realities have coloured many of the subsequent responses to the film.

In her work on Irish national cinema, Ruth Barton contrasts Margot Harkin's *Hush-a-Bye-Baby* (1989) and Orla Walsh's *The Visit* (1992) with *The Snapper*, which she finds seriously wanting:

The radical ambitions of Harkin's and Walsh's films may be usefully contrasted with the adaptation of Roddy Doyle's securely paternalistic and patriarchal novel of the same name *The Snapper* (Stephen Frears, GB, 1993). Set in a lower middle-class estate, Frears' film does not deal with issues of nationalism but rather contemporary social anxieties over teenage pregnancy. When Sharon (Tina Kellegher) announces that she is pregnant, the family rallies around, loudly abusing those neighbours who dare to pass judgement on their offspring. In the absence of a father for the child, Mr Curley (Colm Meaney) steps in and the bad father (a hapless local middle-aged husband played by Pat Laffan) is thrown out and replaced by a good father. This process is made particularly clear in the scenes when Mr Curley begins to show an interest in the pregnancy, furtively scurrying around the public library to hunt out manuals on the female body, through to his whole-hearted involvement in the event. In effect, the pregnancy becomes his and the threat of the single mother bringing up her child in a non-paternalistic family unit is dispelled.[61]

Lance Pettitt, for his part, notes the context of the film and the fact that abortion is not considered as a serious option for Sharon Curley. He worries at the implications of the upbeat ending for future interpretations of the film: 'Doyle's screenplay allowed a mainstream Irish audience to laugh at uncomfortable areas of contemporary experience. Outside this context, however, the representation of Sharon's family is liable to be viewed indiscriminately as a working class family muddling through chaos but coming out well from it.'[62] Even an enthusiastic advocate of the film adaptations of Doyle's novels such as Martin McLoone is uncomfortable with the apparent benevolence of the film's outcome: 'There is, inevitably, an element of wishful thinking in the manner in which Dessie becomes involved in his daughter's pregnancy and in the general air of good-natured solidarity within the family that the film proposes.'[63] The presentation of the film as a comic classic heightens suspicion as if such a serious topic could lend itself to comic treatment without raising serious questions about the ethical nature of the enterprise.

In a scene which takes place in the kitchen in the novel and is transposed to the garden in the film, Veronica (Kay [Ruth McCabe] in the film) asks Jimmy Rabbitte Sr whether they should tell the twin girls that what Sharon did was wrong and that 'they should only have babies when they're married'. Jimmy, who is made uncomfortable by the conversation, uses a phrase which will be repeated in the film by Dessie (Colm Meaney): 'Time's changed.'[64] The drama of the film rotates around the fact that in many respects Dessie is mistaken. Times have not changed as much as all that. And yet, at another level, his platitudinous comment is articulating an important truth not only about himself but about the society around him. Again, what is significant is that the rapid liberalisation of Irish society in the latter half of the 1990s is sketched out and anticipated in the film but that there is no sense that the emergence of more enlightened approaches to moral and social issues can be taken for granted.

When Sharon tells her parents that she is pregnant, it is Dessie who moots the idea of an abortion through the euphemistic phrase, 'D'yeh want to keep it?' (which, in the novel, we are told 'he'd heard a good few times on the telly'[65]). It is his wife Kay who interprets the usually plain-speaking Dessie into intelligible prose by telling Sharon that he wants to know if she wants an abortion. In the film, Sharon declares that 'no way' was she going to terminate her pregnancy. In the novel her refusal is expressed in more stridently ideological terms, where she uses a slogan that was common currency in Pro-Life campaigns in the 1980s:

–There's no way I'd have an abortion, said Sharon.
–Good. You're right.

 –Abortion's murder.

 –It is o' course.[66]

The 'abortion's murder' has all the ring of a borrowed phrase in the mouth of Sharon and is omitted from the film. However, her desire to go through with the pregnancy cannot be seen as a form of complicity with Catholic social teaching or as an easy option favoured by the circumstances of a loving and unconventional family. In many respects, the film of *The Snapper* is a much darker work than the novel on which it is based and the bleakness of Sharon's predicament is repeatedly emphasised through recourse to techniques specific to the medium itself.

Much has been made, for example, in commentary on Roddy Doyle's writing of the descriptive minimalism and the creation of character through spoken language alone. Stephen Frears has spoken of his own attraction to the ability of Doyle's language to summon into being an entire world and community. These characteristics are indeed evident in the tight scripting of the comic exchanges in the film between Dessie and his drinking mates and Sharon and her friends in the Cedar Lounge. However, what is notable in *The Snapper* is the number of occasions when the characters do not, in fact, speak. A technique which is used repeatedly throughout the film is for the camera to move slowly into a close-up shot of the face and it is the movement of the eyes and facial expression which betray feeling or emotion. For example, when Sharon learns that the man who is the father of the child, George Burgess (Pat Laffan), has left the family home, it is the camera capturing the movements of her face and not anything that she says which reveals the degree and nature of her alarm (Plate 7). In a sense, this visual translation is the inevitable outcome of secrecy. If the circumstances of the conception of the child and the conflicting emotions the situation gives rise to are difficult or dangerous to put into words, then the camera is charged with the task of revelation. The close-ups of Sharon's friends reacting

Plate 7. Sharon learns of George Burgess's departure

to the news of her pregnancy, the rapid cross-cutting between the faces of the neighbours commenting on her being with child in the surreal scene where they crowd into her room and appear from under her bed, and a later scene where each of Dessie's drinking mates appears in single succession, close up, again reacting to more news about how the child was allegedly conceived, show how the pregnancy is deeply disturbing for Sharon, her family and the wider community. The trauma in the film version is literally in your face. But this is not simply a question of close-ups, cross-cutting, low-angle shots and altered lighting, which bring in elements of the sinister and the problematic. In one scene in the film, on seeing George Burgess, Sharon panics and rushes back to her house. She hammers frantically on the door and eventually gets in, only to collapse in the hallway. When Dessie walks in, moments later, he steps over his prostrate daughter, ignoring her, and goes to the kitchen to make tea. In the novel, the scene involves George Burgess's daughter, Yvonne, and Sharon's father is not involved in any way. Similarly, scenes involving the butchers in the supermarket ridiculing Sharon on being made pregnant by Burgess, a young shoplifter calling her a 'slut' and her brother Craig (Eanna Mac Liam) being arrested by the police after breaking the front windows of George Burgess's house do not feature in the novel, but their appearance in the film repeatedly emphasise the high social price that Sharon has to pay for her decision.

Indeed, one of the ironies which is stressed in the film is that it is those in positions of authority (Burgess is manager of the local schoolboy soccer team) and who make ostensible display of their religious faith who turn out to be the most ethically abusive. In a long take in the film before Sharon visits the Burgess family home to talk to George Burgess, the camera lingers on a piece of furniture with the telephone on the lower shelf and a standing silver crucifix on the upper shelf (Plate 8). This is something of an establishment shot for the public piety of Burgess. The contrast with the Curley household, where religious iconography is totally absent, is striking. More evidence of Burgess's religiosity is a verbal tic which recurs

Plate 8. The telephone table in the Burgesses' house

throughout the film and is mimicked mercilessly by Dessie, namely, 'on the Bible', an expression Burgess generally uses when he is lying. Thus, rather than giving succour to conventional religious piety, the film, through the character of Burgess, portrays religiosity in society as offering comfort to the abusers rather than the abused.

The filmmaker Johnny Gogan in his review of the film sees it as a facile sit-com rather than as a serious work of art. Part of his argument is that, true to the sit-com approach, the film avoids cinematic drama and that the tension in the central relationship between Sharon and her father is resolved within 'five minutes'.[67] The claim is simply not sustainable on the basis of the film, where, rather than the dramatic conflict being dispensed within minutes, it lasts for the greater part of the film. An important contributory factor to the continuation of hostilities is the fall-out from the scene where Dessie feels particularly aggrieved that his wife and daughter do not appreciate his traditional male defence of wronged womanhood through pub violence. When Dessie does come to terms with Sharon's situation, such has been the force of negativity manifest both within and without the family to Sharon that it is clear that the 'good-natured solidarity' is a fragile vessel and that the 'threat of the single mother' is such that a whole series of tragic and painful events (violence, marital breakdown, physical and mental suffering, social exclusion) are set in train by it, events that undermine rather than shore up a patriarchal status quo.

As Fintan O'Toole has pointed out, a feature of Dessie's character in *The Snapper* is a capacity for change.[68] Throughout the film he grapples with changing definitions of maleness (for example, the taboo on the public expression of emotion in the form of crying) and the calling into question of traditional assumptions about being what Jimmy Rabbitte Sr calls in the novel 'head of the fuckin' house'.[69] The difficulty in response to change is to deem only changes for the worse as worthy of attention. In other words, in the hermeneutics of suspicion, which is often the default value for treatment of social issues on the screen, the fact that a character might actually change for the better and adopt a more progressive attitude to the events unfolding goes against a general prescriptivism of misery. In this view, that an individual might move to a more enlightened position is either part of a malign plot to retain power while appearing to surrender it or an exercise in easy sentimentalism, where you feel good but nobody else has reason to. In effect, what this form of prescriptivism proposes is a wholly static view of history (nothing can really change or if it does it is a maudlin illusion), which is as reactionary as the conservative ideology of an eternal golden age of moral propriety which is forever threatened by changes in society.

One of the changes which greatly preoccupied Irish society in the latter half of the twentieth century was changing attitudes to sexuality, and sexual repression alongside religion would be a recurrent trope in the representation of Ireland on screen.[70] Gogan sees *The Snapper* as another example of the genre, claiming that, 'While the film has its origins in British TV drama it is full of Irish (Catholic) hang-ups about sex being dirty'.[71] Quite the opposite case can be argued, on the basis of the structure and content of the film, and indeed *The Snapper* is an important film precisely because it breaks with the dolefulness and prudishness that characterised much previous representation of Irish sexuality on screen. For example, one of the most common devices in the film is to cross-cut between Dessie and his male friends in conversation and Sharon and her friends talking and joking amongst themselves. In the first scene where we encounter Sharon's friends, they frankly discuss sexual matters, particularly Jackie's recent relationship with Greg, and it is clear that they are very much in control of their sexual lives. They reverse usual role behaviour by Jackie being the one who reaches out and grabs the lounge boy for an order as they comment admiringly on his physical attributes. The point is not that reversal *per se* is necessarily useful or liberatory, one set of sexual stereotypes imitating another, but that throughout *The Snapper*, whether it be Sharon out carousing with her friends or her detailing the delights of the imaginary Spanish sailor to her friend Jackie, there is no inhibition in speaking about and analysing the sexual. It is the hypocrisy of Burgess, who flinches when Sharon uses words like 'hole' and 'knickers' in her confrontation with him in his own home, that reveals the dangerous duplicity of the moral majority. The Burgess who recoils in disdain on the screen at Sharon explicitly describing what happened was not only willing to take advantage of her comatose state to have intercourse with her (an act to which she did not consent, as her drunkenness meant she did not know what was going on) but he himself uses derogatory slang with his drinking mates, calling Sharon a 'great little ride'. It is precisely because the film is not 'full of Irish (Catholic) hang-ups about sex being dirty' that it is Burgess who emerges as the pathetic villain of the piece, as it is he rather than Dessie or Lester (Brendan Gleeson) or Craig who has the sexual hang-ups. *The Snapper* is notable for allowing the young women to talk openly about their sexual lives on the screen and thus show changing attitudes in the society. However, it is neither naïve nor wishful in assuming that social change is a painless process and that there are not always more exploitative elements in the society willing to turn the situation to their own advantage.

In his assessment of Stephen Frears' work, as we noted earlier, David Brown draws attention to Frears' knowledge of the English class system and the manner in which this has informed his cinematographic output. How then does the film cope with a different country and a different society with a different history? Are questions of Irish social class marginalised because the film is financed and directed and produced by outsiders to the vagaries of the Irish class system? The attendant danger in the representation of social class is that a particular social class is presented in a one-dimensional fashion so that their role is largely to confirm stock expectations and comic stereotypes. In situating the film in predominantly working-class Barrytown, the film shows both the internal class complexity of the area and also the relationship between the different social classes within the larger society. Given the importance of spoken language in the construction of the novel, it is hardly surprising that differences in language and in language use are to the fore in the narrative of the film. What is striking is the extent to which the film itself is a repeated exercise in translation as the characters attempt to make sense in their own language of realities which are articulated in another.

In one scene on the DART where Sharon is reading a book she has bought on pregnancy, a voiceover in her own voice talks about 'infected discharge from the vagina' and Sharon looks up from the book and exclaims, 'Jesus, me Fanny!' In a later scene, Dessie is appalled at Sharon talking about her 'bladder pressing on her uterus' and claims that he wants none of that kind of language in the house. 'Piss' translated as 'urine', 'snottiness' translated as 'hormonal imbalance' are further examples of the contrast between the formal language of the text and the vernacular language of the Curleys and the other inhabitants of Barrytown. At one level, of course, these translation techniques are a stock comic device in the film, deflating the sanitised pomposity of literacy with the earthy immediacy of morality. At another, however, they display the manner in which language is there as a barrier in the society, a marker of social class and professional status. Sharon's friends get great comic mileage out of the question put to her in the hospital about her 'menstrual history' (her friend Jackie says, 'Menstrual history, I got a C in that in me Inter'), but Sharon's incomprehension is as much evidence of exclusion through language as it is of creativity in verbal response to her confusion. The language difference is not only articulated through choice of word or linguistic register. Nobody in a position of authority in the community and beyond has the same accent as Sharon or her father or siblings. The availability of sound in film provides the director, of course, with a powerful medium in which to chart social tension through this use of accent. Sharon's supervisor in the supermarket, the policeman in the Garda station who takes sandwiches for Craig, the nurses and doctors in the hospital, all speak with accents that are markedly different from that of Sharon and her friends and family. The accents become in effect the audible soundtrack of authority. Many of the accents are from outside Dublin, mirroring an old antagonism between the functionaries of the new state largely drawn from rural backgrounds and legitimised by the nationalist sanctification of the land and the urban, working-class population, who were largely excluded from any position of power in the new dispensation.[72] The fact, however, that Kay Curley speaks with an accent from outside the city prevents the film from setting up a naïve city/country divide with a binary cast of (city) angels and (country) villains. If authority sounds different, the difference is more of a threat than an opportunity. From the scene in the Rotunda where Sharon asks the nurse whether she herself has had any 'movements' (again language difference as a marker of estrangement) to the fraught encounter between Dessie and the police officer on duty in the station, where the close-ups on the face of policeman (Jack Lynch) and Dessie show the intensity of mutual dislike, the various agencies of the State are feared rather than liked and the mistrust is reciprocal.

In the novel, when Sharon plucks up the courage to see George Burgess, she looks in at the hall while she is waiting for him to come out of the kitchen: 'It was a small hall, exactly the same as theirs. There were more pictures in this one though, and no phone.'[73] In some ways, Sharon's comments are in keeping with the descriptive economy of Doyle's prose, where his preference is for character development and scene evocation through dialogue or internal spoken monologue rather than a Dickensian riot of descriptive detail. In Frears' film, however, the differences in the Burgess and Rabbitte households are soon made evident. Burgess's son, Pat (Denis Menton), answers the door in a school uniform, whereas the schoolgoing Curley children are never shown in uniform. There is a phone in the hall and the crucifix we commented on earlier, and as the scene moves to the front room of the house the camera shows us floral wallpaper, an aquarium with exotic fish and more expensive-looking dark furniture. The two families live across the road from each other but what the forensic sweep of the camera reveals is that they inhabit different social worlds, with the Burgesses displaying all the outward signs of lower middle-class ambition. Not only does George Burgess have a different accent from the Curleys but, when his wife Doris Burgess wants to express her dismay and anger at the turn of events, she breaks that quintessential symbol of social aspiration, the white, porcelain teapot. This dramatic gesture filmed in the large, well-equipped, empty modern kitchen shows the vulnerability not only of her position in the relationship but the uncertainty of the family's social ascent. The cinematographic medium is used to great effect in the Burgess household to stress the internal class complexity and tensions of the Barrytown community. *The Snapper* does not offer an idyllic image of a timeless working-class community who, smiling through it all, are united in their triumph over adversity. The different practices, aspirations and behaviours of neighbours living in very close proximity show the very real tensions generated by the differing class ambitions of the residents of Barrytown.

In the early years of Irish independence a primary motive for the legislation on the censorship of cinema was the belief that cinema itself constituted a grave threat to indigenous Irish culture. The State set itself the cultural task of promoting native language, sport and culture as a means of counteracting what was seen as the ever-present menace of international popular culture, whether it was through the medium of moving pictures or jazz music. The latter half of the twentieth century saw the gradual dismantling of the repressive cultural apparatus of censorship and the advent of television, single and multi-channel, opened up the living rooms of the nation to the news from elsewhere.[74] So, if *The Snapper* gives an account of changing social mores in Ireland, what does it tell us about changing cultural identities? Is there anything that is culturally specific to the Curleys or would they be indistinguishable, for example, from a similar working-class family in England watching them on British television, where the film was first broadcast to record audiences? Lynda Myles, the producer of both *The Snapper* and *The Van*, has commented on the ability of *The Snapper* to reach audiences in very many different cultures:

> The Japanese, for example, loved the films and *The Snapper* was among the top twenty in France that year. It was nominated for a Cesar, and in Spain won the Premio Goya as best European film. I can't explain how it works but Roddy does have this gift for striking the same basic chord in everyone. Whether it's love of family or love of laughter I just don't know.[75]

Is there a sense in which this facility of identification is based on a lack of cultural particularism or is there a form of cultural identity made available in *The Snapper* which thrives on a particular version of the particular?

The television is an important presence in *The Snapper* and, when Dessie is not in the pub, he is frequently shown alone or with other members of the family watching a variety of programmes on the television. Kay Curley is happy enough to have sex with Dessie once she does not have to miss *The Antiques Roadshow*. Scenes are introduced with a close-up shot of television images (as with the scenes from a yachting race) before the camera pulls back to reveal Dessie or the rest of the family in the living room. In one scene, Dessie zaps between different channels looking for a suitable programme to watch. One television image that the camera dwells on for a number of seconds is that of a hurling match and then, as Dessie zaps again and the shot switches to Dessie, we hear Irish music on the soundtrack coming from a programme we cannot see. An irate Dessie then casts the remote control aside saying there is 'nothin' on the telly'. His impatient dismissal of two emblems of Irish cultural distinctness could be interpreted as evidence of a hostility to any form of separate cultural expression, a feeling of alienation from activities that were co-opted into the nation-building project by the indigenous bourgeoisie and whose perceived exclusivism holds little attraction for Dessie in the predominantly working-class suburb of Barrytown. His passion, shared by his family, for the popular culture of Anglo-American television would suggest that they feel no particular affinity for the official cultural heritage of their island home.

The film, however, usefully complicates any facile opposition between a predatory international popular culture and a native culture that heroically resists the blandishments of the modern and the urban. After Sharon announces the news of her pregnancy to her family, she and her father decide to go to the pub. We then have an exterior shot and relatively long take of Kimberley Curley (Ciara Duffy) going through a majorette's routine, twirling a baton to the sound of the song 'Molly, my Irish Molly' (Plate 9). The scene is somewhat unusual coming after the kitchen-sink drama of what has gone before. But in a sense, what we have is another way of signalling

Plate 9.   Kimberley Curley as majorette

55

the extent to which cultural change is taking place in ways not scripted by cultural purists. Here we have not one of the Irish dance routines that appears in *The Commitments* but a form of dance largely associated with American popular culture. The tune, however, is Irish-American, made popular by De Danann, who did much to reintroduce Irish audiences to the music composed and performed by Irish emigrants who had gone to the United States.[76] What characterised the music was not only the encounter with other forms of ethnic music but also the influence of the technologies of amplification and recording. These recordings in turn would affect the development of traditional music in Ireland itself. So the scene with Kimberley is a condensation of the constant traffic between home and away, between the popular culture of the folk tradition and the popular culture of the entertainment industry, and the Curleys in their own way straddle these different cultures. In yet another example of the prefigurative potential of the film, what the majorette scene signals is the hybrid resources of the culture that will lead the following year to the *Riverdance* phenomenon, with its particular mix of the Hollywood chorus line and traditional Irish step-dancing.[77]

The fusion of different cultures and influences is announced indeed from the outset of the film when the film title and credits appear with no images but a version of the Elvis song, 'I can't help falling in love with you'. The version is by Spin the Tops and is strongly influenced by the London-Irish sound produced by The Pogues in their breakthrough albums of the period. Again, we have American popular culture meeting emigrant Irish culture (this time from England) and producing a sound that is distinctive in its mixity. It is in many ways entirely appropriate that it is cinema (and television), two powerful vectors of popular culture, which allow for the expression of the emergence of new forms of Irish popular culture and not least of the ironies is that this is done by an English director for a British television audience. Rather than going for the readily available cultural icons of Irish difference (religion, Gaelic games, Irish dance), Frears puts on screen the cultural realities of the lives of the Barrytown community in which the hallowed borders of national distinctiveness have little purchase but where novel ways of imagining culture are coming into being. To the extent that this situation is one that is prevalent in many parts of the world as the result of the ascendancy of the mass media and the growing interconnectedness of people's lives globally, then it is the very *hybridity* of the culture that makes it *distinctive*. In other words, identification is facilitated by elements of international popular culture (television viewing, global images of US culture) but the specific mixture (elements of Irish local and diasporic cultures) means that the hybridity is inflected in a specific way. So there is identification (perception of commonality) and recognition (perception of difference) and one does not annul the other.

In seeking out elements of commonality, Linda Myles speculates that 'love of family or love of laughter' may have explained the international success of *The Snapper*. It is, of course, the Rabbitte/Curley family which provides an important element of continuity between the three films of the trilogy, although it is unquestionably *The Snapper* where family is most persistently the focus of the filmmaker's attention. The change in name from *The Commitments* and the novel was due to Alan Parker having a contractual right to use the name Rabbitte in any subsequent films. Part of the drama of *The Snapper* is that it is not simply that a new child is to be born but that many of the characters are themselves being born into something different. The gestation of the child is also the transformation of the lives of various members of the Curley household. We have already seen the genesis of a new kind of Dessie as his traditional notions of maleness and male status are challenged. It is his daughter too, however, who not only gives birth to a child but is born into a new self as the film progresses. This change in Sharon is emphasised in the film through a visual contextualisation which is not available in the novel. For example, the opening scene of the film has the sound of invisible children quarrelling and a bedroom door slowly opens to reveal Sharon feeling her stomach and looking at it in a wardrobe mirror. On the door – and we will see this again in subsequent shots – is a sign saying 'Caution Children'. At the height of the tension between Sharon and Dessie there is a scene shot again in the bedroom where the camera slowly pans the bunk beds and the soft toys before revealing Sharon once more looking at her stomach in the mirror. Sharon shares the room with her two younger sisters, Kimberley and Lisa (Joanne Gerrard), and so in a sense shares the lingering world of childhood that they inhabit. The camera visually reinforces this sense of belonging through the accumulation of contextual detail and the number of scenes shot in the shared bedroom.

As the pub scenes with Sharon's friends demonstrate, neither she nor they are blushing maidens locked into an infantilised fantasy world of innocent and sexually naïve females, but her knowingness does not make the final transition from childhood through the liminal state of adolescence to adulthood any easier. In the scene in George Burgess's front room where he offers Sharon some money, he first tells her to buy 'sweets' with it and then quickly corrects himself and says 'drinks'. His tacit admission of her in-between state makes his own behaviour all the more heinous, but it is further evidence of the fraught journey that Sharon has to make to an adulthood which is contested by others. The journey is, however, to do with beginnings rather than endings, and in this respect represents a decisive break with a tradition of representing Ireland on screen, from *The Dawn* (1936) to *The Crying Game* (1992), which places the experience of the Irish and Ireland under the sign of death. That this should be so is perhaps hardly surprising in view of a militaro-political conflict that claimed over 3,000 lives. The force of a domestic political tradition in which the notion of sacrifice and martyrology was to the fore and the influence of external perceptions exclusively mediated through the prism of bloody conflict meant that variations on death, decline, defeat, and failure were often the preferred mode of dealing with the Irish on screen.

Mary Condren detects a much older tradition at work in Irish culture where, she argues, a death-centred patriarchal culture of Christian sacrifice ousted an earlier matricentral culture centred on the giving of life through birth rather than death.[78] By situating the film within the context of birth, genesis and generation, Frears and Doyle are liberating their Irish subjects from the endless waking of the dead. The sense of the rejection of a death-oriented culture is not only manifest in the choice of childbirth as a subject matter to be celebrated but is also apparent in a whole set of scenes which are interpolated into the film and which do not figure in the novel, namely the return of Craig from his tour of duty as a UN peacekeeper with the Irish army. In a later scene, in the pub, Craig's friends are incredulous when he tells them that the guns they used abroad as part of their duties had 'no bullets'. His friends cannot see the point of guns without bullets, but Craig argues that it is through the moral force of their presence and their unflinching courage in difficult situations (they look any potentially hostile elements straight in the eye and try to 'mesmerise' them) that they manage to keep the peace.

Craig then is a soldier who is living rather than dying for Ireland so that others might live. He and his comrades go out not to bring death but life to the communities they are entrusted to protect. So these are guns being mentioned in an Irish context but this time without bullets, guarantors of peace rather than agents of warfare. Again, the inclusion of the whole UN episode, and Ireland's international association with peace as opposed to war, further strengthens the radical embrace of life and birth as the productive metaphors for the film's enterprise. If the owl of Minerva in Hegel's opinion generally flew at dusk and finitude has certainties that forecast lacks, the freshness and boldness of *The Snapper* is in part to do with the courageous uncertainty of any moment of generation. And it is in this respect that *The Snapper* is a key document in any history of Ireland in the latter half of the twentieth century. Between the publication of the novel and the making of the film, Irish society is already entering the period of accelerated change which will make it a very different place at the end of the decade from the beginning.[79] In the early years of the 1990s a new society and a new country is being born but, as with any birthing of the new, precisely because it is new and unlike what has gone before, it is unrecognisable. Dessie and Sharon and Kay, and not only the 'snapper', are being born into new circumstances. If Dessie repeats again to Sharon, in the scene when he talks about the birth of his own children, what he has said earlier to Kay, namely that the 'times have changed', it is a comment as much on the country in which they live as on the particular circumstances of parenting in the Curley family. Thus, the film captures that particular moment when a society emerges, albeit with great difficulty and with much hesitation, into a moment of difference, when life is ultimately affirmed and the tantalising romance of death finally repudiated.

If Doyle was to entitle one of his later works *The Woman Who Walked Into Doors*, doors opening and closing are a recurrent structural device in the film. From the first scene which opens with an opening door to the careful shutting and opening of doors in the Burgess household to the repeated slamming of doors in the Curley home, doors are repeatedly framed by the director's camera. Doors are, of course, as much a way in as a way out and, in a film where characters spend a great deal of their time trying to get out of certain difficult situations and make their way into more tolerable circumstances, the door becomes a key motif of concealment and revelation. In the crowded household of Curleys the door also comes to represent the very tenuous threshold between the public and the private as Sharon tries to keep the younger children out of the private space of her grief and her parents attempt to bracket their decision-making from the promiscuous mayhem of the crowded house. There are exterior shots of Sharon crossing O'Connell Street after buying her book on pregnancy from Easons, Sharon on the DART, Craig coming down the steps of the DART and walking towards home, but much of the film is shot either within the domestic space of home or the confined public space of the Cedar Lounge. Hence, as in the theatre, the door becomes an important dramatic device for a narrative change, whether it is Dessie going downstairs from the lounge (world of young female drinkers) to meet his friends (older, male drinkers) or Lisa entering the sitting room and being reprimanded by her father for going out in a short black dress, the tension indicative of further changes to happen in the family. The duality of the door as a structuring device echoes Frears' penchant for structural parallelism in the construction of cinematographic metaphor. After the birth of his grandchild, Dessie races to the pub across the road and orders a pint. To his right is seated a rather forlorn-looking drinker to whom Dessie simply says, 'seven pounds, twelve ounces' (Plate 10). His bar-stool companion then asks, po-faced, whether he is referring to a baby or a turkey. This scripted metaphorical parallel between turkey and baby finds a visual

Plate 10. Dessie at the bar after the baby is born

equivalent, this time between grandfather and grandchild, when Dessie is shown downing his celebratory pint in double-quick time and burping, an image which is intercut with shots of Sharon feeding Georgina (Alannagh McMullen) and rubbing her gently to release wind. Given the difference in budget and scale from a film like *The Commitments* and the general background of television drama, the artful employment of parallelism is an effective use of visual resources to set up a field of resonance which goes beyond the scenes themselves and allows for suggestive analogies (the maturity of Sharon/the infantilisation of Dessie) to be worked out on screen and in the eyes and minds of the audience.

The Ireland which Doyle and Frears put on the screen in *The Snapper* does not have the aesthetic alibi of artistic creation (there is no heroic tale of a music group being formed) or the post-colonial glamour of revolt (there is no revolutionary manifesto being articulated for the transformation of the Dublin working class), but this does not mean that the film lacks ambition. In dealing with a more restricted set of characters than *The Commitments*, and in concentrating in particular on the relationship between Sharon and her father, *The Snapper* is able to explore in considerable depth the forces for change which are reworking the society from the bottom up. In making the personal political rather than the political personal (the thrust of *The Commitments*), Frears and Doyle show that putting Ireland into film does not only mean tracking the birth of a new society but it also implies the birth of a new way of imagining Ireland as it moves into the global neighbourhood of Barrytown.

4

THE VAN (1996)

The ends of trilogies like the sequels of blockbusters can invite scepticism as much as disappointment. Fintan O'Toole hints obliquely at the less than enthusiastic response to *The Van* in his plea for taking the three films of the Barrytown Trilogy as an aesthetic whole rather than as discrete parts:

> it is only when they are taken together that the world in which they happen acquires, through the characters, the rich texture that the visual style avoids. The quietest of the films, *The Van*, is the most dependent on the accumulated resources of the other two and, if it is viewed in isolation from them, it seems rather small and flat.[80]

O'Toole is right to signal important continuities between the *The Van* and the other two films in the trilogy, but it would be a mistake to underestimate the particular qualities of the second film directed by Stephen Frears and where Roddy Doyle himself is author not only of the novel on which the film is based but also of the screenplay. In the production notes to the film, Frears in fact sees *The Van* in explicitly cinematographic terms precisely because it is not 'rather small and flat': 'The only difference between then [*The Snapper*] and now is the scale. *Snapper* was a small, simple, moving story. *The Van* is altogether bigger, huge in comparison, and that's why we are making it for cinema, not TV.'[81] The scale can be taken literally in terms of the actual expansion in location, with the bulk of the film shot in Kilbarrack but with beach scenes shot at Dollymount Strand and additional films and exteriors built at Ardmore Studios in Wicklow.

The van itself as an agent of mobility has the characters move around and outside their area. First, it literally brings them to the other side of the DART tracks to find the van, then it is led in ceremonial procession to Bimbo's (Donal O'Kelly) home. Later, powered by diesel rather than brawn, the van makes the journey to Dollymount Strand and in the end the same strand becomes the destination on its final journey to abandonment. But there is arguably a further sense in which the film is 'altogether bigger' and that is its explicit connection to a story of Ireland as seen on film. There is a thematic condensation which brings into particularly sharp focus the sense of the film's historical context as a liminal period in recent Irish history. *The Snapper* was focused primarily on one family, the Curleys, and involved the necessary interface with neighbours and friends. *The Van* moves us out of family into a world which is concentrated on friendship and on the more extended relationships between the protagonists, Larry (Colm Meaney) and Bimbo, and the wider community. These extended relationships enjoy more prominence, partly because of the very nature of the business they are engaged in (selling fast food to the local community) and also because Ireland's World Cup successes in 1990 became a local and national rather than a purely private event. Thus, although the Rabbitte/Curley family provide a strong element of continuity in the trilogy, particularly in the person of actor Colm Meaney, who plays the role of the family patriarch in all three films, it would be mistaken to see the three films as variations on the family-driven television serial, as the role of family is markedly different in all three.

As if to stress the change in scale, the film of *The Van* opens not in the quiet of the Rabbitte house, where Jimmy Sr in the novel 'had the kitchen to himself',[82] but in the Fox Hunter pub, where Larry and his drinking partners hear a tearful Bimbo tell them that he has lost his job. The camera cuts from a head and shoulders shot of crying Bimbo (Plate 11) to the wider community of drinkers at the bar. The individual predicament in the novel becomes a collective one in the film, just as the initial focus on Bimbo rather than Larry, whose literary counterpart Jimmy Rabbitte Sr is the main narrative voice, destabilises an overly

Plate 11. Bimbo in tears

facile identification of *The Van* as yet another episode in a family sitcom. Bimbo as a friend rather than family member means that the relational patterns are going to be different, if no less fraught. The specific cinematographic tradition that acts as a template for the exploration of this type of relationship as opposed to the familial is the 'buddy movie'. Frears explicitly acknowledged this antecedent and refers to *The Van* as an 'unemployment buddy movie', claiming that, as he was making the film, 'I was constantly thinking of *The Odd Couple*, Jack Lemmon, Walter Matthau, in Ireland.'[83] Doyle himself, while confessing that he had not initially thought of *The Van* as a buddy movie, stated that, 'as the script developed we began to think of it as *Butch Cassidy and the Sundance Kid*. And before we were through we were openly referring to it as "Thelma and Louise With Chips"'.[84] Of course, what characterises both *Butch Cassidy and the Sundance Kid* (dir. George Roy Hill, 1969) and *Thelma and Louise* (dir. Ridley Scott, 1991) is that they are 'buddy movies' in which the buddies very definitely move.

If the camera has long enjoyed a romance with mobility, it has partly been because the camera has brought images of mobility and elsewhere to the immobile.[85] *The Van* flags this affinity in a number of allusions that have no parallel in the novel. In one of the earliest scenes in the film we get a close-up of a picture of John Wayne on a wall of the Curley household, *Where in the World?* is the first television programme referred to in the film and when the van is towed to the car park of the Fox Hunter, Larry (Colm Meaney) is framed in a shot saying, 'Take him to Missouri, ma'am!'. So not only are the buddies taken out of their families but they are also in a sense taken out of their familiar environments or find themselves in unfamiliar positions in familiar surroundings. Instead of being on the inside of the pub drinking with their friends, Larry and Bimbo find themselves on the outside giving them something to eat. Whereas Jimmy Sr is pleased to find he has the kitchen to himself, his cinematographic incarnation Larry finds that he and Bimbo have become the kitchen for the local community. It is Larry not his wife who now wears the apron, in a reversal of gender conventions, and a place of leisure now becomes a place of work as Dollymount Strand is turned into a halting-site of commercial opportunity.

As the title ironically suggests, *The Van* is a particular kind of road movie, not only because the film itself includes explicit reference to the cinematographic tradition of mobility in the Western and is situated in the context of the more mobile versions of the buddy movie genre but because the vehicle of transformation is the vehicle itself. The van as focus of attention means that we have a particular kind of dwelling in travelling, where, as it moves from pub to beach to concert, the microcosm of the 'kitchen' with the accompanying knot of relations remains as the world outside changes from minute to minute. In a sense, this is kitchen sink drama for the screen, as the kitchen sink is not rooted immutably to one spot but changes location as the van pursues its seasonal customers. In the novel it is television which provides Jimmy Sr and much of the rest of the family with their window on the world. As Jimmy notes to himself in one of the introspective passages of the novel, 'he watched Sky News in the day.

He couldn't keep up with what was happening these days, especially in the Warsaw Pact places. They were talking about it one day, him and Darren and Sharon and Veronica, and even the twins, at their dinner.'[86] The television information historically situates Jimmy and his family at a moment of significant change, not only, as it turns out, for Ireland but for the rest of Europe as well. In the film these references to precise continental historical events are omitted, as is a very early domestic political reference in the novel to the release of the Guildford Four. Television will indeed play a significant role in the film, as we shall see, around the event of the World Cup itself. However, it can be argued that in the film it is the 'hatch' in the chipper van which acts as Larry's and Bimbo's window on their world.

As the large number of hatch-centred shots in the film show, it is through the screen of the hatch that Larry and Bimbo, alongside Diane (Neilí Conroy) and to a lesser extent Kevin (Ruaidhrí Conroy), both view events unfurl before them and are themselves framed for the outside world. In the manner in which films projected onto the screen of a railway carriage window were a form of entertainment for Dubliners at the turn of the last century, giving them the illusion of travel,[87] the hatch of the van becomes a screen on the screen where Larry, Bimbo and Larry's children observe everything from a country transformed by soccer success to the increasing ferocity of street violence in communities undermined by unemployment and social deprivation. There is even the added sensation of the van being rocked by local hoodlums paralleling the rocking motion applied to the static railway carriages in the amusement arcades of yore to enhance the feeling of physical displacement. If they can't 'quite keep up with what was happening' in their community, it is because the small screen of the hatch as much as the small screen in Jimmy Rabbitte's house is framing a world in transition. The difference between the small screen of home and the small screen of work is, of course, that in the case of the latter they are not only the watchers but the watched. Larry and Bimbo are not only supplying food to hungry customers but Larry in particular is also providing entertainment and the film provides numerous instances of Larry's verbal bravado on the moving stage of the hatch, from the child looking for a choc ice to the disgruntled customer complaining about the nappy in batter that has been inadvertently sold to him. Thus, we as viewers end up not only observing Larry's performance but the performance of the audience watching the performance. In effect, the film is structured around a series of inside/outside oppositions – inside the house/outside the house, inside the stereotype (Larry as Patriarch)/outside the stereotype (Larry as Matriarch), inside the screen (performance)/outside the screen (spectatorship) – where the constant inversions and reversals are analogous to a place and a community looking for bearings in a country and a world where things happen fast and not just on the screen.

The inside/outside dichotomy is also played out in the representation of the relationship between writer, actors and director. In defending his decision to return to Kilbarrack to shoot *The Van*, Stephen Frears asks, 'Why should we change? This was Barrytown exactly as he Roddy Doyle described it. The community he knew first hand.'[88] Doyle himself confirms this image of the insider with privileged knowledge with his claim that he 'lived and worked in a suburb exactly like Barrytown' and that such was his proximity to his subject that 'I had to protect the identity of the people I was living among' by imagining the name 'Barrytown' for his fictional suburb.[89] The validation of role by personal experience is also highlighted by Colm Meaney, who sees acting in the film as part of an autobiographical journey, a journey facilitated by the documentary fidelity of Doyle's writing: 'I was born and bred in an area like Barrytown. That's what makes these roles such a pleasure to play – it's like going back to your childhood. And Roddy has drawn even the most minor characters with such accuracy you feel you're shaking hands with old friends.'[90] A potential difficulty with this self-representation is that it gives sustenance to a naïve literalism of the aesthetic, where the camera simply records what is happening and dutifully brings the unexceptional everyday to the big screen. Doyle in his interview with Liam Fay describes his impatience with those who see his writing as a form of reportage, where he is simply seen as a clever stenographer who goes around recording people's conversations and then produces the novel or the screenplay as the written record. He says of his work, 'It's a distinctive style and it's deceptively simple.'[81] So the insider as witness must become an outsider as writer if there is any way in which shape in the form of characterisation, plot or narrative is to be given to the material that is being offered to the reader or viewer.

If Doyle and Meaney are offered up as exemplary insiders, Stephen Frears on the other hand is presented as a worthy outsider. Donal O'Kelly, who acts the part of Bimbo in the film, argues that 'that innocent outsider's eye he [Frears] is able to bring to the film is a priceless asset'.[92] Being an outsider is not necessarily an unquestioned virtue and of course part of the argument for an indigenous Irish cinema over the years has been to free insiders from the representational tyranny of outsiders. Fintan O'Toole, for example, points to the dangers of facile exoticism when the green get to the screen, a problem compounded by the further barrier of social class dividing many filmmakers from their working-class subjects: 'Implicit in this situation is a further sense of distance. Not only is there a gulf of class, there is also the gulf of nationality. There is, potentially, a double layer of exoticism: the thrill both of looking into lives and looking into Irish lives.'[93] Frears as the director of a previous version of a Doyle novel is presumably not as 'innocent' as O'Kelly would want us to believe, but it is notable that the film studiously avoids iconic images of the land or religion, two staples of the filmic representation of the Irish by foreign directors. For example, in the scenes shot near Dollymount Beach – with the sole exception of the last shot in the film of the stranded van – there are no long, slow, wide-angle, panoramic shots to frame the film within the readily available visual grammar of the touristic. John Wayne is pictured on screen, not the Sacred Heart nor the Virgin Mary. The image of the suffering but compassionate Irish matriarch is readily deflated by the harassed mother on Dollymount beach who, on the screen of the hatch, tells Larry that what he describes as her 'lovely' children are bastards and that she hopes that the child she is expecting will be born deaf and dumb. Frears, in a sense, is the outsider that lets insiders present the world in their own terms rather than in the terms dictated by other outsiders. In the process, the outsider becomes a kind of insider, a fact he acknowledges by claiming that, whereas initially 'I had all the typical Englishman's fears and preconceptions about the Irish', by the time he came to make *The Van* it was like 'going back home'.[94]

Frears was not the only Englishman, of course, to get involved with the Irish. Jack Charlton as manager of the Irish soccer team during the 1990 World Cup was another. In the context of the continuing military conflict in Northern Ireland, this conjunction of an English manager and an Irish team made up of many English-born players had its own particular resonance. Part of the inevitable change in scale that was mentioned at the outset of the chapter relates to the framing of a national event within the context of the lives of the Barrytown community. Ger Ryan, who plays the role of Maggie, Bimbo's wife, described the World Cup year of 1990 as 'brilliant, four million people partying day and night' and that it 'was Ireland packing up its troubles and throwing the biggest ceili [*sic*] in history'.[95] As a key event in the film the soccer World Cup is not an innocent object of the medium's attention. If Gaelic football and hurling had long been associated with representations of Irishness and feature as a kind of visual signature tune for Irish specificity on the screen, soccer as a 'foreign game' was less fortunate. In addition, it was a game associated with cities and former garrison towns like Sligo and Athlone, largely played by the urban working class, so in the traditional nationalist imaginary it was triply suspect.

In the novel there is an extended scene where Jimmy Sr goes to watch his son Darren play for Barrytown Utd Under-18s and another where Jimmy Sr and Bimbo get to act as stewards at an Ireland–Wales match in Landsdowne Road. Neither of these scenes feature in the film, so we are not offered any sense of continuity between the role of soccer as a community activity, the practice of a particular social class and the community's enthusiasm for the game on the screen. Instead, the film takes its cue from another sentence in the novel, where the narrator simply states: 'The country had gone soccer mad.'[96] Barrytown on the screen becomes Ireland on the streets, a metonym for the 'four million people partying on the streets'. The madness is partly accounted for in the film itself by the sharp contrast between the harsh reality of unemployment and an attendant sense of failure, notably articulated in the scene where Larry and Mary in a tense exchange discuss what to do about Christmas presents, and the euphoria of national soccer success on a world stage. The novel is not sparing in its description of the psychological and social damage of unemployment, but the film – beginning with Bimbo's announcement of job loss – is even more insistent on the debilitating effects of economic depression.

If 'Ireland was packing up its troubles', the troubles were not only economic: the troubles were also the Troubles, the long, protracted reality of military and political conflict on the island. Ireland's footballing success is good for business as Larry and Bimbo capitalise on the empty stomachs of the fans, but is it good for politics? Here the film has to deal with an apparent paradox. The 'foreign game' is in fact foreign to few countries on earth and, as the very name of the tournament suggests, the World Cup is a global event. However, what characterises the response of the inhabitants of Barrytown to the universal game is an explosion of national fervour. In the words of the film's costume designer, Consolata Boyle, 'In pride of our little country, the Irish were rediscovering innocence and naïvete [*sic*] which went back to childhood. They were showing off, which we do rather well.

We were wearing anything . . . so long as it was green.'[97] At one level, Consolata Boyle's comments elaborate on the carnival atmosphere around the games and the holiday from more mundane realities signalled by the fancy dress of green paraphernalia. At another, they are indicative of a nostalgia for a more uncomplicated sense of national belonging, the pre-Troubles 'innocence and naivete' which did not automatically equate tricolours and symbols of nationhood with armed conflict and the deadly attrition of political strife. The 'pride of our little country' brings not the tears of heartbreak and mourning but tears of joy to the eyes of Larry and his drinking mates.

History, of course, does not take leave of the stage so easily. The two games which are featured at length in the film are the game against Romania, which takes Ireland through to the quarter finals, and the game against England. The latter game, which ends in fact in a draw, is interpreted as a glorious victory by the Barrytown locals and in a later scene in the film Larry wears a 'Britbusters' T-shirt in homage to the result. In the film, once the match is over, Weslie (Brendan O'Carroll) stands above the crowd and declaims, 'Maggie Thatcher! Winston Churchill! Elton John! Fuck You!' (Plate 12) and the post-match pub scene finishes to the strains of the nationalist anthem, 'A Nation Once Again'. The scene is similar to one in the novel where Bertie loudly excoriates a number of famous English men and women. However, in the novel, the singing of 'A Nation Once Again' occurs not after the English but after the Romanian match and is not the work of anonymous drunken singers but is initiated by the generally reviled Larry O'Rourke. When he starts to sing, the immediate, ironic comment from an unidentified drinker is, 'Ah, somebody shoot tha' fucker!'[98] This more irreverent approach to nationalist orthodoxy is omitted from the film and the sense of explicit opposition between the two countries is heightened by the juxtaposition of the England game and the Irish patriot song and the generalisation of the song to overall soundtrack (thus becoming communal) rather than being identified with any one

Plate 12. Weslie and post-match euphoria

single individual. It is possible to interpret these scenes as evidence of a latent resentment and political hostility which is never far from well-policed surfaces. Conversely, the collaboration of an English director and Irish writer in constructing the post-match scene could be seen as evidence of the universality of play, redirecting the more destructive energies of particularism into the partisan iconography of green jerseys and verbal banter and away from the killing fields of empire and nation. In a sense, Frears and Doyle take the more courageous option of directly depicting the raucous Anglophobia of the Barrytown locals rather than opting for a carefully sanitised version of events and showing how historical tensions do not always have to be represented on screen in the fraught language of political violence.

For the vast majority of the 'four million people partying on the streets' the 1990 World Cup was a screen event. In the film, as at the time, many people went to watch the games in local pubs, so that the experience of watching television became a communal event and in this respect was closer to a cinematographic experience than a televisual one. During the English and Romanian matches the large screen of the cinema zooms in on the small screen of the television set, so that the cinema audience of *The Van* find themselves in an analogous position to the pub audience of Barrytown. The film incorporates the images of the matches into its own narrative but the marked difference in the quality of the image between the shots of the pub crowd and the shots of the televised game visually mark the distance which is, of course, always there between the game on the screen and the crowd in the Fox Hunter. The film can present images that the novel must describe but it is no less conscious of the need to frame these images in a particular way and situate the audience in relation to them.

In the interplay between text and film, a striking feature of *The Van*, with respect to the other two novels in the trilogy, is the extent to which cinema itself is a crucial element in the construction of identity in the text. One of the central characters in the novel, Bertie (the local wide boy who will become Weslie in the film), speaks in the mock Spanish accent of the parodic Western. In one typical exchange, Bertie claims not to know who a group of drinkers are in the corner of the pub, saying, 'Don't know, compadre, said Bertie. – Gringos'.[99] The very language which Bertie speaks is the language of the cinema and reader's recognition of this presupposes a familiarity with the intertext of the cinematographic. When the Barrytown residents come out to jeer at Jimmy Sr and Bimbo pushing their engineless van towards Bimbo's house, Jimmy Sr reflects: 'There really was a huge crowd out. It was a bit like Gandhi's funeral in the film, except noisier.'[100] It is to cinema that his thoughts again turn when the van is under attack from the Living Dead, the neighbourhood hooligans: 'It was like that film, *Assault on Precinct 13*, and the van was Precinct 13.'[101] *Gandhi* (dir. Richard Attenbourgh, 1982), *Assault on Precinct 13* (dir. John Carpenter, 1976) and *Holocaust 2000* (dir. Alberto De Martino, 1977) are among the explicit cinematographic references, with the film *Cocktail* (dir. George Donaldson, 1988) providing the template in the novel for an extended song-and-dance routine performed by Jimmy Sr and his son in the back garden of the family home. Cinema is not somehow out there as a discrete leisure activity but is an integral part of how the principal narrative voice (Jimmy Sr) construes events and how elements of characterisation (Bertie) are realised in the novel. As an important constituent of urban popular culture, it is to cinema that Jimmy Sr looks when he seeks a metaphorical frame for particular experiences, whether this be a reaction to crisis or an expression of joy. Although literature is not absent from the novel, with references to Hopkins, Alexandre Dumas, William Golding and Charles Dickens, and with a host of references to television programmes and advertisements, it is cinema that is explicitly invoked as a way of making sense of specific experiences. There is a strong sense in *The Van* that the text which goes into film has already, in a way, come out of film. The cultural materials that the fictional inhabitants of Barrytown use to construct their world are in many instances taken from the general store of Anglo-American popular culture, of which cinema is a significant element. The manner in which experience is mediated is not through the inherited pieties of a national literacy but through the international audio-visual culture of generations thoroughly acculturated to the different forms of visual media. In this respect, it is entirely understandable that *The Van* should make it on to the screen as part of the dialogue with cinema which the writer has already initiated on the pages of the novel.

If the success of the Irish on the playing fields of Italy bolsters the self-confidence of the local community and fills the till of the chipper van, the parable of transformation is not only to do with a country whose fortunes are suddenly beginning to change for the better. The two main female characters, Maggie (Ger Ryan) and Mary (Caroline Rothwell), are in their different ways important agents of change. Maggie not only supports Bimbo's venture after the camera shows her initial hostility on seeing the dilapidated van, but she goes on to be the organising genius behind the enterprise, fixing up Bimbo and Larry with permits and outlets for their catering activities. One of the earliest scenes in the film is of Mary, Larry's wife, reading *Silas Marner* by George Eliot. She is studying English for the Leaving Certificate and in a later scene she announces her excellent result to a strongly hung-over Larry. Business acumen and educational ambition are ways in which the women seek to change their lives and escape the dual tyranny of social deprivation and gender stereotype.

Fintan O'Toole has commented on the sexual confusion of working-class males towards the end of the twentieth century, 'men being forced by unemployment and loss of economic status to take on female roles'.[102] We see Larry bringing Diane's baby in the stroller to the pitch-and-putt course, washing and cleaning the outside of the van (to cries of 'scrubbers') and later working in the chipper van preparing food and wearing an apron. Activities traditionally associated with females – child minding, housework and cooking – are now the domain of the male characters on the screen. The transition is not without difficulties, however, and much of the dramatic tension in the film centres on the problems that Larry, in particular, experiences with changing roles. In one scene, where Larry is peeling potatoes for chips, there is a tense exchange with Maggie over what concerts the van should go to in their drive to increase business and in the previous scene Larry tells his own wife, Mary, that he believes Maggie is hostile to him. In the novel we are given many more details of Maggie's business schemes, such as providing people with dinners in their own homes and offering commuters breakfasts on their way to work. The film is more elliptical in its evocation of Maggie's business skills, but there is no doubt that her organisational abilities are central to the initial success of the catering enterprise. Larry's growing dislike of Maggie is crucially linked to his perception that she has assumed a position of authority and usurped the traditional male prerogative of command.

The situation is made even more problematic for Larry, in that the role reversal not only takes place at the level of Maggie and himself but at the level of the 'buddies' themselves, who undergo a change which is akin to gender switching. Our first image of Bimbo is of a man in tears, and as he gradually adjusts to his new situation, Larry takes charge of him, bringing him on his outings to the pitch-and-putt course and integrating him into his daily routine. Colm Meaney, commenting on his own role in the film says, 'I've heard *The Van* described as a sort of love story and I'd go along with that. The relationship between Larry and Bimbo is unusual because they're not the sort of guys who think about relationships, if you follow me. But deep down they really care about each other, even though they may not realise it.'[103] In this relationship, Bimbo initially occupies the stereotypical position of the passive, 'emotional' female partner (his very name suggesting a derogatory term for a supposedly simple-minded woman) with Larry as the dominant male, deciding how and in what way they should spend their days. Once the van is acquired, however, and the business starts, Larry's position gradually changes and he increasingly sees himself not as the (dominant) partner but as the (dependent) employee. At one point in the novel, anticipating the cinematographic representation, the narrator comments, 'It was like a film about a marriage breaking up.'[104] The scenes where Larry talks about joining a union and his resolutely observing his entitlement to a lunch break are evidence of his resentment at the change in circumstances, where he is now in the conventional role of the dependent female and the formerly meek Bimbo becomes the irate boss and ruling male. Even in the scene in the Leeson Street nightclub where Larry seeks to reassert his embattled machismo it is the two women, Dawn (Barbara Bergin) and Anne Marie (Charlotte Bradley), who remain firmly in control of the situation. Larry's advances are resolutely resisted and it is Bimbo not Larry who proves the more seductive of the two. In the end, it is Larry who now becomes highly 'emotional' as his anger turns into violence and we have the scene of the fight between Larry and Bimbo, which starts in the van and carries on outside. So not only is Larry's patriarchal authority being challenged from within by his own son, Kevin, but many of the significant relationships in Larry's life are changing. What they have in common is that the former conventional attributes of gender are challenged and that customary notions of maleness are ill-adapted to a community and society that are changing before Larry's eyes. The Odd Couple reveal many kinds of oddity, not the least of which is the imbalance in power relationships between men and women and the more recent historical tendency to construe maleness as a site of emotional self-discipline and coercive control.[105]

The team that lined out for matches in Italy in 1990 was, as we noted earlier, made up of many of the children and grandchildren of Irish emigrants. Doyle notes the affinity between the team and an expanded notion of Irishness: 'You must remember that Ireland's greatest export is people and when their team goes through everyone stands up to take the credit.'[106] The diasporic awareness implicit in Doyle's comments has been a relatively recent phenomenon, as the historical neglect of Irish emigrants in Britain eloquently demonstrates. Prior to Mary Robinson's championing of the Irish diaspora in the 1990s, their role and potential contribution to Irish life was in general ignored, though the diaspora figured prominently in the formative years of Irish nationalism and films such as *The Quiet Man* had explored relationships between the Irish at home and the emigrant other.[107] The Irish soccer team translated the reality of the diaspora into the popular imagination and made notions of belonging more complex than simple geographical position. Notions of what it might mean to be Irish were challenged by the language and accents of footballers who had been born and grew up outside the country. But the challenge to accepted notions of identity did not just result from the encounter with the realities of diasporic identity. As the economic growth of the 1990s gathered momentum, the movement of people became not so much outwards as inwards. It is a development to which Doyle responded by producing a play for the stage featuring Jimmy Rabbitte Sr entitled *Guess Who's Coming for the Dinner* (2001) and becoming a regular contributor to the immigrant publication, *metro eireann*. However, for the purposes of our discussion here, it is worth considering to what extent *The Van* is already beginning to problematise a question that will feature increasingly in Ireland's engagement with film towards the end of the twentieth century, that of native and immigrant identities.

As the crowds pour out of the pub at closing time after the match against England, Larry is shown busily dealing with orders. One customer orders curried chips and Larry's immediate if geographically confused retort is that they don't sell curried chips because 'we're not fuckin' Chinese. This is an Irish chipper.' In an earlier scene when Larry and Bimbo go to a takeaway restaurant we learn that it is Vietnamese and that they had to leave the area of Barrytown before dark because they had bricks thrown at them for being foreigners. Prior to the significant rise in immigration in the mid-1990s, the Vietnamese were numerically the most important immigrant refugee group to arrive in post-independence Ireland.[108] There is no Vietnamese chip van in the novel, so the film is clearly signalling a connection between the economic fortunes of recent immigrants to Ireland and the beginnings of racism. Ironically, what happens to Larry and Bimbo is that they gradually realise that being an 'Irish chipper' is no guarantee against mob violence and that, as their van is attacked by the Living Dead, they become the 'Chinese' or the 'Vietnamese' of the community, the Natives who transmute into Newcomers in the eyes of other Natives.

Larry and Bimbo come to experience what it is to be in the vulnerable position of a group whose presence is more or less tolerated by elements of the community. In the novel it is Jimmy Rabbitte Sr who leaves an Italian takeaway – where he and Bimbo had unsuccessfully tried to find out how chips were made – who shouts, 'Go back to your own country, he said. – Fuck the EEC.'[109] The

Italians as an older immigrant group (novel) and the Vietnamese as historically more recent arrivals (film) are identified as the groups who literally provide sustenance to the community. At one level, in their role as service providers they are more integrated into the community than the corporate anonymity of McDonalds, which in *The Van* is the butt of scorn and ridicule on both page and screen. At another level, as Larry and Bimbo will discover to their cost as they become the new Strangers, their position is always precarious as the community produces those who will bite the hand that feeds them in the name of a prior territorial imperative (we/the Irish/the Living Dead were here first).

If nomadism is classically the condition of the persecuted and the dispossessed – from the Jews to the Romany community – then the chipper van of Larry and Bimbo occupies a critically ambiguous position in the film. On the one hand, the van settles in one location, the car park of the Fox Hunter or Dollymount beach, and here the camera films different groups from the fixed vantage point of the vehicle. This is the temporarily sedentary moment of community engagement. On the other, the van has the potential to move and take flight, as it does when the disgruntled customer on a bicycle is left behind in a series of scenes which evoke the Keystone Cops rather than the high-speed chase of the thriller. Here, the camera moves as location shifts rapidly into dis-location. Thus, as a means of integration and an instrument of flight, the van almost inevitably shapes the outlook of Larry and Bimbo, who find themselves *estranged* from the surrounding community, not only because of their new-found economic status but because, like the refugee or the immigrant, without rights they are always potentially *mobile*, always prepared for exit, whether it be as the result of the forced expulsions of state or the intimidatory violence of ethnic triumphalists ('Go back to your own country'). The most dangerous moment in the film comes, of course, when there is no escape. Here the mob outside bombard the van with missiles and literally attempt to immobilise it. The camera angles show us Larry and Bimbo and Sharon looking down from the heights of the van on the customers outside but increasingly their position makes them less sovereign (privileged observer) than target (the van as conspicuous other), more outside than inside or where the inside (of the van) becomes less of a command post and more of a refuge (from the outside).

Stephen Frears, in his comments on *The Van* and Roddy Doyle, makes the general claim that, 'Whatever the emotion is, anger, grief, frustration, violence, at some unexpected moment it all becomes hilarious. It's very Irish . . . and very Roddy Doyle.'[110] These comments can understandably make Irish critics and viewers nervous. The Irish as lovable rogues (once they keep away from politics) and whimsical geniuses always risks courting condescension while offering a public rhetoric of admiration.[111] Whether hilarity is a peculiarly Irish condition is a moot point and, as the abandoned van is shot from near and then afar at the end of the film to further increase its sense of isolation, it is not immediately obvious in the film that 'at some unexpected moment it all becomes hilarious'. There are, of course, many comic moments in the film and the reputation for the comic that came from *The Snapper* would be used to promote *The Van* on its release in 1996. In a sense, the darker subject matter of *Family* (1994) is already prefigured in the more intractable emotional difficulties faced by Larry, Bimbo and their families in *The Van*.

More significantly, perhaps, *The Van* shows us a community which is not some quaint playground of the comically disaffected but is part of the larger society, which is going through one of the most significant periods of change in post-independence Ireland. Changes in economic activity (the rise of the tertiary sector and the numbers of self-employed – the chipper van, Bimbo), transformed gender roles (Maggie/Mary), new definitions of maleness (Darren the vegetarian/Larry the cook), the decline of institutional religion (notable in its absence from the film) and an increased awareness of Ireland's relationship to the wider world through both its diaspora and an immigrant labour force (soccer and food), and general improvements in educational attainment (Darren's and Mary's Leaving Certificate honours) are all elements of the changed Ireland that makes its way into the film of *The Van*. What is particularly striking in the work of Doyle and Frears is the ability to take a specific historical event such as the World Cup of 1990 and use it as a means of highlighting not only the difficulties (the business fails) but also the capacity for change of a community. The final film in the trilogy is not then a joyous romp that ends in the sweet tragedy of failure but a work which conveys in all its complexity the Ireland that was coming into being in the summer of the beginning of the last decade of the last century.

Notes

1. Liam Fay, 'Never Mind the Bollix!', *Hot Press*, Vol. 17, No. 10 (1993), pp. 39–40.
2. Fintan O'Toole, 'Going West: the Country Versus the City in Irish Writing', *Crane Bag*, Vol. 9, No. 2, pp. 111–116.
3. Cormac Ó Gráda, *The Economic Development of Ireland Since 1870* (Dublin: Centre for Economic Research, UCD, 1993).
4. Michael Cronin and Barbara O'Connor, 'Introduction', in *Tourism in Ireland: a Critical Analysis*, eds. Barbara O'Connor and Michael Cronin (Cork: Cork University Press, 1993), pp. 1–10.
5. Mark J. Prendergast, *Irish Rock: Roots, Personalities, Directions* (Dublin: O'Brien Press, 1987); John Waters, *Jiving at the Crossroads* (Belfast: Blackstaff, 1991); John Waters, *Race of Angels: Ireland and the Genesis of U2* (Belfast: Blackstaff Press, 1994).
6. Farrel Corcoran, *RTÉ and the Globalisation of Irish Television* (Bristol: Intellect, 2004).
7. Martin McLoone, *Irish Film: the Emergence of a Contemporary Cinema* (London: British Film Institute, 2000), p. 205.
8. Fay, p. 39.
9. Lance Pettitt, *Screening Ireland: Film and Television Representation* (Manchester and New York: Manchester University Press, 2000), p. 124.
10. Peter Clinch, Frank Convery and Brendan Walsh, *After the Celtic Tiger: Challenges Ahead* (Dublin: O'Brien Press, 2002), pp. 24–42.
11. Fay, p. 39.
12. Fay, p. 40.
13. Johnny Gogan, Review of *The Snapper*, *Film Ireland*, No. 35 (June/July 1993), p. 24.
14. Alan Parker, 'Note', 'The Tosser's Glossary', press pack for *The Commitments*, 1991.
15. Michael Cronin, *Translating Ireland* (Cork: Cork University Press, 1996), pp. 134–138.
16. Declan Kiberd, *Inventing Ireland* (London: Jonathan Cape, 1995).
17. Timothy D. Taylor, 'Living in a Postcolonial World: Class and Soul in *The Commitments*', *Irish Studies Review*, Vol. 6, No. 3 (1998), p. 298.
18. Taylor, p. 298.
19. See Terence Dolan, *A Dictionary of Hiberno-English* (Dublin: Gill & Macmillan, 1998), and entries for words listed in the 'Tosser's Glossary'.

20. Fintan O'Toole, 'Working-Class Dublin on Screen: the Roddy Doyle Films', *Cineaste*, Vol. XXIV, Nos. 2–3 (1999), p. 38.

21. O'Toole, 'Working-Class Dublin on Screen', p. 38.

22. Taylor, p. 298.

23. For a trenchant critique of the failure of Celtic Tiger Ireland to address social inequality, see Peadar Kirby, *The Celtic Tiger in Distress: Growth with Inequality in Ireland* (London: Palgrave, 2002).

24. For a (critical) summary of the thesis, see the introduction to Conor McCarthy, *Modernisation: Crisis and Culture in Ireland 1969–1992* (Dublin: Four Courts Press, 2000), pp. 11–44.

25. Scott Lash and John Urry, *Economies of Signs and Spaces* (London: Sage, 1994), p. 4.

26. See Stephanie Rains, 'Home from Home: Diasporic Images of Ireland in Film and Tourism', in *Irish Tourism: Image, Culture and Identity*, eds. Michael Cronin and Barbara O'Connor (Clevedon: Channel View Publications, 2003), pp. 196–214.

27. Ulrich Beck, Natan Sznaider and Rainer Winter (eds.), *Global America?: the Cultural Consequences of Globalization* (Liverpool: Liverpool University Press, 2003).

28. James Clifford, *Routes: Travel and Translation in the Late Twentieth Century* (Cambridge, MA: Harvard University Press, 1997).

29. Jan Patočká, 'La Culture Tchèque en Europe?' (1939), in *L'Idée de l'Europe en Bohême*, tr. Erika Abrams (Grenoble: Jérôme Million, 1991), p. 141.

30. Marc Crépon, 'Penser l'Europe avec Patočká. Réflexions sur l'altérité', *Esprit*, No. 310 (2004), p. 33: 'La liberté, en effet, n'est pas dans le repli qui enferme un individu dans l'horizon étroit de sa propre culture – de sa culture en tant qu'elle lui est propre et qu'elle le protège à l'intérieur de ses frontières. La culture est synonyme de liberté, dès lors qu'elle permet de franchir ses frontières en devenant, par un jeu de traductions, de transferts et d'échanges, la culture de tous – et qu'inversement la culture des «autres», devenant la mienne, cesse d'être exclusivement la leur.'

31. Roddy Doyle, *The Commitments* (Dublin: King Farouk, 1987), p. 129.

32. Alan Parker, 'Some Notes on the Making of the Film', production notes, *The Commitments*, 1991, p. 3.

33. 'The Making of *The Commitments*', DVD, 20th Century Fox Home Entertainment, 2000.

34. Alan Parker's filmography includes: 1973: *Our Cissy; Footstep;* 1974: *No Hard Feelings;* 1975: *The Evacuees* (TV); 1976: *Bugsy Malone;* 1978: *Midnight Express;* 1980: *Fame;* 1982: *Shoot the Moon; The Wall – Pink*

Floyd; 1984: *Birdy*; 1986: *A Turnip's Head Guide to the British Cinema*; 1987: *Angel Heart*; 1989: *Mississippi Burning*; 1990: *Come See the Paradise*; 1991: *The Commitments*; 1994: *The Road to Wellville*; 1996: *Evita*; 1998: *Angela's Ashes*.

35. David Thomson, *The New Biographical Dictionary of Film* (London: Little, Brown, 2002), p. 666.

36. Pettitt, p. 124.

37. Taylor, p. 297.

38. Doyle, *The Commitments*, pp. 7–8.

39. Taylor, p. 293.

40. See Niall Ó Dochartaigh, *From Civil Rights to Armalites: Derry and the Birth of the Irish Troubles* (Cork: Cork University Press, 1997).

41. Therese Caherty (ed.), *Is Ireland a Third World Country?* (Belfast: Beyond the Pale Publications, 1992).

42. O'Toole, 'Working-Class Dublin on Screen', p. 37.

43. Parker, 'Some Notes on the Making of the Film', p. 4.

44. Brian Guckian, review of *The Commitments*, *Film Base News*, No. 25 (1991), p. 18.

45. Doyle, *The Commitments*, p. 92.

46. Parker, 'Some Notes on the Making of the Film', p. 5.

47. Parker, 'Some Notes on the Making of the Film', p. 3.

48. O'Toole, 'Working-Class Dublin on Screen', p. 37.

49. Parker, 'Some Notes on the Making of the Film', p. 5.

50. Paul Sweeney, *The Celtic Tiger: Ireland's Economic Miracle Explained* (Dublin: Oak Tree Press, 1998).

51. Doyle, *The Commitments*, p. 22.

52. Doyle, *The Commitments*, p. 98.

53. *The Commitments*, production notes, p. 20.

54. Parker, 'The Making of *The Commitments*'.

55. Pettitt, *Screening Ireland*, p. 126.

56. Taylor, p. 300.

57. Fay, p. 39.

58. 1967: *The Burning* (short); 1971: *Gumshoe*; 1972: *A Day Out* (TV); 1973: *England Their England* (TV); 1973: *Match of the Day* (TV); 1974: *The Sisters* (TV); 1975: *Sunset Across the Bay* (TV); 1975: *Three Men in a Boat* (TV); 1975: *Daft as a Brush* (TV); 1976: *Play Things* (TV); 1976: *Early Struggles* (TV); 1977: *Eighteen Months to Balcolmbe Street* (TV); 1977: *Last Summer* (TV); 1977: *Able's Will* (TV); 1977: *Black Christmas* (TV); 1977: *A Visit from Miss Protheroe* (TV); 1978: *Cold Harbour* (TV); 1978: *Me! I'm Afraid of Virginia Woolf* (TV); 1978: *Doris and Doreen* (TV); 1978: *Afternoon Off* (TV); 1978: *One*

Fine Day (TV); 1979: *Bloody Kids* (TV); 1979: *Long Distance Information* (TV); 1981: *Going Gently* (TV); 1982: *Walter* (TV); 1983: *Walter and June* (TV); 1983: *Saigon – Year of the Cat* (TV); 1984: *The Hit*; 1985: *My Beautiful Laundrette*; 1986: *Song of Experience*; 1987: *Prick Up Your Ears*; 1987: *Sammie and Rosie Get Laid*; 1988: *Dangerous Liaisons*; 1990: *The Grifters*; 1992: *Hero*; 1993: *The Snapper*; 1994: *A Personal History of British Cinema by Stephen Frears* (TV); 1996: *Mary Reilly*; 1996: *The Van*; 1998: *The Hi-Lo Country*; 2000: *High Fidelity*; 2000: *Fail Safe* (TV); 2001: *Liam*.

59. Fay, p. 39.
60. Thomson, p. 314.
61. Ruth Barton, *Irish National Cinema* (London: Routledge, 2004), p. 120.
62. Pettitt, *Screening Ireland*, 2000, p. 124.
63. Martin McLoone, *Irish Film*, p. 205.
64. Roddy Doyle, *The Snapper* (London: Secker and Warburg, 1990), p. 49.
65. Doyle, *The Snapper*, p. 6.
66. Doyle, *The Snapper*, p. 6.
67. Johnny Gogan, Review of *The Snapper*, *Film Ireland*, No. 35 (1993), p. 24.
68. Fintan O'Toole, 'Family Solidarity', *Irish Times* (10 April 1993), p. 13.
69. Doyle, *The Snapper*, p. 46.
70. Tom Inglis, *Moral Majority: the Rise and Fall of the Catholic Church in Modern Ireland*, second ed. (Dublin: University College Dublin Press, 1998); Kevin Rockett, *Irish Film Censorship: a Cultural Journey from Silent Cinema to Internet Pornography* (Dublin: Four Courts Press, 2004).
71. Gogan, p. 24.
72. Fintan O'Toole, *The Southern Question* (Dublin: Raven Arts Press, 1987).
73. Doyle, *The Snapper*, p. 84.
74. See Farrel Corcoran, *RTÉ and the Globalisation of Irish Television* (Bristol: Intellect, 2004).
75. *The Van*, production notes, 1996, p. 11.
76. See Fintan Vallely (ed.), *The Companion to Irish Traditional Music* (Cork: Cork University Press, 1999).
77. Barbara O'Connor, 'Riverdance', in *Encounters with Modern Ireland*, eds. Michel Peillon and Eamonn Slater (Dublin: IPA, 1998), pp. 51–60.

78. Mary Condren, *The Serpent and the Goddess: Women, Religion and Power in Celtic Ireland* (New York: Harper & Row, 1989).
79. Michael Cronin, 'Changing Times, Changing Cultures', in *Ireland and the European Union: the First Thirty Years, 1973–2002*, ed. Jim Hourihane (Dublin: Lilliput Press), pp. 12–25.
80. O'Toole, 'Working-Class Dublin on Screen', p. 38.
81. *The Van*, production notes, 1996, p. 9.
82. Doyle, *The Van* (London: Minerva, 1992), p. 1.
83. *The Van*, production notes, pp. 9–10.
84. *The Van*, production notes, p. 14.
85. Charles Musser, 'The Travel Genre in 1903–1904: Moving Towards Fictional Narrative', in *Early Cinema: Space – Frame – Narrative*, ed. Thomas Elsaesser (London: British Film Institute, 1990), p. 127.
86. Doyle, *The Van*, p. 69.
87. See Michael Cronin, 'Moving Pictures: Kate O'Brien's Travel Writing', *Ordinary People Dancing: Essays on Kate O'Brien*, ed. Eibhear Walshe (Cork: Cork University Press, 1993), pp. 137–149.
88. *The Van*, production notes, 1996, p. 9.
89. *The Van*, production notes, 1996, p. 12.
90. *The Van*, production notes, 1996, p. 15.
91. Fay, p. 38.
92. *The Van*, production notes, 1996, p. 15.
93. O'Toole, 'Working-Class Dublin on Screen', p. 36.
94. *The Van*, production notes, 1996, p. 8.
95. *The Van*, production notes, 1996, p. 17.
96. Doyle, *The Van*, p. 176.
97. *The Van*, production notes, 1996, pp. 18–19.
98. Doyle, *The Van*, p. 182.
99. Doyle, *The Van*, p. 32.
100. Doyle, *The Van*, p. 119.
101. Doyle, *The Van*, p. 189.
102. O'Toole, 'Working-Class Dublin on Screen', p. 39.
103. *The Van*, production notes, p. 14.
104. Doyle, *The Van*, p. 292.
105. See Gavan Titley, *Youth Work with Boys and Young Men as a Means to Prevent Violence in Everyday Life* (Budapest: Council of Europe, 2003).
106. *The Van*, production notes, 1996, p. 12.
107. Seán Cronin, *Washington's Irish Policy: 1916–1986: Independence, Partition, Neutrality* (Dublin: Anvil Books, 1987); Luke Gibbons, *The Quiet Man* (Cork: Cork University Press, 2002).

108. Tanya Ward, *Asylum Seekers in Adult Education: a Study of Language and Literacy Needs* (Dublin: City of Dublin VEC and County of Dublin VEC, 2002).

109. Doyle, *The Van*, p. 133.

110. *The Van*, production notes, 1996, p. 11.

111. See Joep Leerssen, *Mere Irish and Fíor-Ghael: Studies in the Idea of Irish Nationality, its Development and Literary Expression Prior to the Nineteenth Century* (Amsterdam: John Benjamins, 1986).

CREDITS

Title:	The Commitments
Director:	Alan Parker
Release Year:	1991

Cast:

Robert Arkins	Jimmy Rabbitte
Michael Aherne	Steven Clifford, Piano
Angeline Ball	Imelda Quirke, Backup Singer
Maria Doyle Kennedy	Natalie Murphy, Backup Singer (as Maria Doyle)
Dave Finnegan	Mickah Wallace, Drums
Bronagh Gallagher	Bernie McGloughlin, Backup Singer
Félim Gormley	Dean Fay, Sax
Glen Hansard	Outspan Foster, Guitar
Dick Massey	Billy Mooney, Drums (quit)
Johnny Murphy	Joey 'The Lips' Fagan, Trumpet
Kenneth McCluskey	Derek Scully, Bass
Andrew Strong	Deco Cuffe
Colm Meaney	Jimmy Rabbitte Sr
Anne Kent	Mrs Rabbitte
Andrea Corr	Sharon Rabbitte
Gerard Cassoni	Darren Rabbitte
Ruth Fairclough	Rabbitte Twin
Lindsay Fairclough	Rabbitte Twin
Michael O'Reilly	Greg
Liam Carney	Duffy
Ger Ryan	Pawnbroker
Mark O'Regan	Father Molloy
Phelim Drew	Roddy Craig the Reporter
Sean Hughes	Dave Machin from Eejit Records
Philip Bredin	Ray
Aoife Lawless	Imelda's Sister
Lance Daly	Kid with Harmonica
Conor Malone	Protest Song Singer
Jezz Bell	Heavy Metal Singer
Colm Mac an Iomaire	Fiddler Auditioner

Emily Dawson	Punk Girl Singer
Dave Kane	Coconuts Trio
Kristel Harris	Coconuts Trio
Maria Place	Coconuts Trio
Brian Mac Aodha	Uileann Pipe Player
Tricia Smith	*Les Misérables* Singer
Canice William	Smiths' Song Singer
Patrick Foy	Cajun Trio
Allan Murray	Cajun Trio
Jody Campbell	Cajun Trio
Eanna Mac Liam	Failed Drug Buyer
Philomena Kavanagh	Rabbittes' Neighbour
Peter Rowan	Shy Skateboard Auditioner
Eamon O'Connor	'Only De Lonely' Singer
Maura O'Malley	Joey's Mother
Blaise Smith	Pool Hall Manager
Derek Herbert	Duffy's Sidekick
Owen O'Gorman	Duffy's Sidekick
Pat Leavy	Unemployment Official
John Cronin	Kid with Horse
Rynagh O'Grady	Bernie's Mother
Sheila Flitton	Church Cleaner
Michael Bolger	Community Centre Kid
Mick Nolan	Imelda's Father
Eileen Reid	Imelda's Mother
Bob Navan	Regency Pub Barman
Derek Duggan	Photographer
Paddy O'Connor	Rock Salmon Man
Jim Corr	Avant-Garde-A-Clue Band
Larry Hogan	Avant-Garde-A-Clue Band
Bernard Keelan	Avant-Garde-A-Clue Band
Ronan Hardiman	Dance Hall Manager
Mikel Murfi	Music Journalist
Josylen Lyons	Deco's Fan
Winston Dennis	Man in Limousine
Alan Parker	Eejit Record Producer
Paul Bushnell	Eejit Engineer

Rest of cast (listed alphabetically)

Caroline Corr	Extra (uncredited)
Sharon Corr	Fiddle Player (uncredited)

Mark Leahy	Wedding Guest (uncredited)
Martin O'Malley	Young Priest (uncredited)

Credits:

Alan Parker	Director
Roddy Doyle	Original Novel
Roddy Doyle	Screenplay
Ian La Frenais	Screenplay
Dick Clement	Screenplay
Marc Abraham	Co-producer
Armyan Bernstein	Executive Producer
Dick Clement	Co-producer
Souter Harris	Executive Producer
Ian La Frenais	Co-producer
Lynda Myles	Producer
Roger Randall-Cutler	Producer
Tom Rosenberg	Executive Producer
David Wimbury	Line Producer
Gale Tattersall	Photography
Gerry Hambling	Film Editing
John Hubbard	Casting
Ros Hubbard	Casting
Brian Morris	Production Design
Arden Gantly	Art Direction
Mark Geraghty	Art Direction
Karen Brookes	Set Decoration
Penny Rose	Costume Design
Peter Frampton	Makeup Supervisor
Aaron Glynn	Hair Stylist
Laurie Borg	Production Manager
Paul Barnes	Third Assistant Director
Cliff Lanning	Third Assistant Director
Adam Lee	Trainee Assistant Director
Belinda McCullagh	Trainee Assistant Director
Gerry Toomey	Second Assistant Director
Mick Walsh	Co-Second Assistant Director
Bill Westley	First Assistant Director
Tommy Allen	Property Master
Tommy Bassett	Construction Manager
Paul Fleming	Standby Painter
Linda Hederman	Art Department Assistant

Pascal Jones	Standby Rigger
Nuala McKernan	Standby Prop
Vivion O'Brien	Standby Carpenter
Eamonn O'Higgins	Dressing Props Master
Jimmy O'Meara	Standby Stagehand (as James O'Meara)
Ronnie Skinner	Property Buyer
Derek Wallace	Chargehand Prop
Robbie Adams	Assistant Engineer
Jack Armstrong	Boom Operator
Gregg Barbanell	Foley Artist
Allan Brereton	Boom Operator
Clayton Collins	Sound Editor
Terry Cromer	Multi-track Crew
Julian Douglas	Multi-track Crew
Leonard Green	Assistant Sound Editor
Eddy Joseph	Supervising Sound Editor
Kevin Killen	Music Mixer
Tim Martin	Set Recording Engineer
Chuck Michael	Foley Editor
Andy Nelson	Sound re-recording mixer
Joe O'Herlihy	Sound consultant
Steve Pederson	Sound re-recording mixer
Tom Perry	Sound re-recording mixer
Jim Phelan	Multi-track Crew
Ted Swanscott	ADR recordist
Clive Winter	Sound Mixer
Maurice Foley	Special Effects
Edward J. Adcock	Second Camera Operator
David Appleby	Still Photographer
Cate Arbeid	Production Coordinator
Libbie Barr	Script Supervisor
Ciarán Barry	Camera Trainee
Peter Bloor	Gaffer
Conor Brady	Musician
Fran Breehan	Musician
Dan Breen	Action Vehicles
Gary Burritt	Negative Cutter
Allen Burry	Publicist
Paul Bushnell	Music Arranger
Dale Caldwell	Color Timer

Carolyne Chauncey	First Assistant Editor
James Cozza	Second Assistant Editor
Valerie Craig	Production Coordinator
Con Dempsey	Chargehand Electrician
Dermot Diskin	Second Assistant Editor
Ronan Dooney	Musician
Rachel Fallon	Casting Assistant
Jessica Felton	Casting Assistant
Eamonn Flynn	Musician
Barbara Galawan	Music Liaison: Dublin (as Barbara Galavan)
Brendan Galvin	Clapper Loader
Carl Geraghty	Musician
Amy Hubbard	Production Assistant
John Hughes	Music Co-ordinator
Patrick Isherwood	Production Accountant
Jim Jolliffe	Camera Trainee
Eddie Knight	Best Boy
Hugh Linehan	Location Assistant
Sarah Lucraft	Assistant Accountant
John Maguire	Camera Trainee
Alan McPherson	Best Boy
Stewart Monteith	Rigging Gaffer
Lisa Moran	Assistant to Alan Parker
Tara Mullen	Production Assistant
John Murphy	Grip
Anneliese O'Callaghan	Production Assistant
Eamonn O'Keeffe	Focus Puller
Martin O'Malley	Location Manager
Maeve Paterson	Wardrobe Mistress
Mike Roberts	Camera Operator (as Michael Roberts)
G. Marq Roswell	Music Supervisor (as G. Mark Roswell)
Reuben Seid	Production Assistant
Libby Shearon	Publicist
Isobel Stephenson	Second Assistant Editor
Ann Stokes	Wardrobe Assistant
Sophie Thornley	Assistant to Producers
Robert Walpole	Location Assistant
Ian Weatherly	Wardrobe Assistant

	(as Ian Weatherley)
Janty Yates	Wardrobe Supervisor
Mary Montiforte	Production Accountant (uncredited)
Sam Montiforte	Post-production Accountant (uncredited)

Title:	The Snapper
Director:	Stephen Frears
Release Year:	1993

Cast:

Colm Meaney	Dessie Curley
Tina Kellegher	Sharon Curley
Ruth McCabe	Kay Curley
Eanna Mac Liam	Craig Curley
Peter Rowan	Sonny Curley
Joanne Gerrard	Lisa Curley
Colm O'Byrne	Darren Curley
Ciara Duffy	Kimberley Curley
Fionnuala Murphy	Jackie O'Keefe
Dierdre O'Brien	Mary
Karen Woodley	Yvonne Burgess
Pat Laffan	George Burgess
Virginia Cole	Doris Burgess
Denis Menton	Pat Burgess
Brendan Gleeson	Lester
Ronan Wilmot	Paddy
Stuart Dunne	Bertie
Dylan Tighe	Boy 1
Caroline Boyle	Girl 1
Jennifer Kelly	Checkout Woman
Audrey Corr	Customer, Neighbour 3
Stanley Townsend	Anaesthetist
Cathy Belton	Desk Nurse
Miriam Kelly	Doctor
Eleanor Methven	Dr. Cook
Birdy Sweeney	Loner (as Birdie Sweeney)
Barbara Bergin	Midwife
Billie Morton	Midwife 2
Joan Sheehy	Woman in Hospital
Rynagh O'Grady	Neighbour 1

Sheila Flitton	Neighbour 2
Cathleen Delaney	Oul'one
Ailish Connolly	Nurse
Jack Lynch	Policeman
Stephen Kennedy	Supermarket Trainee Manager
Britta Smith	Woman in Police Station
Conor Evans	Barrytown Neighbour
Helen Roache	Barrytown Neighbour
Marie Conmee	Barrytown Neighbour
Jimmy Keogh	Barrytown Neighbour
Aisling Conlan	Baby Curley
Alannagh McMullen	Baby Curley 2
Tom Murphy	Pal 1
Robbie Doolin	Pal 2
Matthew Devereux	Young Lad/Dad
Sandy	Famine

Credits:

Alan Parker	Director
Roddy Doyle	Original novel
Roddy Doyle	Screenplay
Ian Hopkins	Associate Producer
Lynda Myles	Producer
Mark Shivas	Executive Producer
Oliver Stapleton	Photography
Mick Audsley	Film Editing
Leo Davis	Casting
Mark Geraghty	Production Design
Jean Kerr	Art Direction
Consolata Boyle	Costume Design
Morna Ferguson	Makeup Artist
Jennifer Hegarty	Makeup Artist
Mary Alleguen	Production Manager
Melanie Dicks	Production Manager
Fiona Murray	Production Manager
Martin O'Malley	First Assistant Director
Robert Walpole	Third Assistant Director
Mick Walsh	Second Assistant Director
Suzanne Nicell	Trainee Assistant Director (uncredited)
Russ Bailey	Settings

Nuala McKernan	Set Dresser
Eamonn O'Higgins	Props
Noel Walsh	Props Trainee
Mick Boggis	Dubbing Mixer
Paul Delaney	Boom Operator
Dan Gane	Dubbing Editor
Kieran Horgan	Sound Recordist
Peter Joly	Dubbing Editor
Peter Maxwell	Dubbing Mixer
Steve Hancock	Sound Camera Operator (uncredited)
Tina Brophy	Administration Staff
Alan Butler	Focus Puller
Frances Byrne	Administration Staff
Mary Casey	Assistant Editor
Tom Collins	Still Photographer
John Conroy	Clapper Leader
Anne Dunne	Head Dresser
Penny Eyles	Script Supervisor
Mary Finlay	Assistant Editor
Donal Geraghty	Administration Staff
John McDonnell	Location Manager
Rhona McGuirke	Costume Assistant
Niall O'Meachair	Location Manager
Larry S. Prinz	Gaffer
Luke Quigley	Grip
Alan Williams	Administration Staff
Colin Coull	Color Grader (uncredited)

Title:	The Van
Director:	Stephen Frears
Release Year:	1996

Cast:

Colm Meaney	Larry
Donal O'Kelly	Brendan 'Bimbo' Reeves
Ger Ryan	Maggie Reeves, Bimbo's Wife
Caroline Rothwell	Mary, Larry's Wife
Neilí Conroy	Diane, Larry's Daughter
Ruaidhrí Conroy	Kevin, Larry's Son
Brendan O'Carroll	Weslie, Fox Hound Regular

Stuart Dunne	Sam
Jack Lynch	Cancer
Laurie Morton	Maggie's Mum
Marie Mullen	Vera, Weslie's Wife
Jon Kenny	Gerry McCarthy, Fox Hound Regular
Moses Rowen	Glenn Reeves
Linda McGovern	Jessica Reeves
Eoin Chaney	Wayne Reeves
Frank O'Sullivan	Wally, in Parked Car with Girl
Jill Doyle	Mona
Barbara Bergin	Dawn, Nightclub Girl
Charlotte Bradley	Anne Marie Nightclub Girl
Ronan Wilmot	Bald Man with Nappy
Stanley Townsend	Des O'Callahan, DES Health Inspector
Sheila Flitton	Missis Twix
Alan King	Myles the Mechanic
Bernie Downes	Pregnant Woman Customer
Martin Dunne	Garda Sergeant
Tommy O'Neill	Nightclub Barman
Eilish Moore	Bingo Woman
Paul Raynor	Pitch & Putt Man
Eileen Walsh	Crushed Girl
Sandra Bagnall	Complaining Woman
Fionnuala Murphy	Young Woman (as Fionuala Murphy)
Michael O'Reilly	Arsenal Supporter
David Kelly	Choc Ice Boy (1st Customer)
Lee Bagnall	Crying Boy
Jamie Bagnall	Other Kid
David Byrne	Barry
Gavin Kelty	World Peace (as Gavin Keilty)
Claude Clancy	Leo, Fox Hound Barman
Michelle Gallagher	Girl
Arthur Napper	Nightclub Bouncer
Jessie O'Gorman	Kerrie, Diane's Baby Girl

Credits:

Stephen Frears	Director
Roddy Doyle	Original novel

97

Roddy Doyle	Screenplay
Mary Alleguen	Line Producer
Lynda Myles	Producer
Mark Shivas	Executive Producer
Roddy Doyle	Co-producer (uncredited)
Eric Clapton	Original Music
Richard Hartley	Original Music
Oliver Stapleton	Cinematography
Mick Audsley	Film Editing
Leo Davis	Casting
Mark Geraghty	Production Design
Fiona Daly	Art Direction
Consolata Boyle	Costume Design
Anne Dunne	Key Hair Stylist
Morna Ferguson	Key Makeup Artist
Jennifer Hegarty	Assistant makeup artist: Winter Unit
Olwyn Lee	Trainee Makeup Artist
Martina McCarthy	Assistant Hair Stylist
Marian Barlow	Makeup Artist
Miriam Coleman	Trainee Assistant Director
Martin O'Malley	First Assistant Director
Willie Smith	Third Assistant Director
Russ Bailey	Construction manager
Clodagh Conroy	Assistant Art Director
Richard Curley	Stagehand
Conor Devlin	Draughtsman
Jason Doherty	Carpenter
Pascal Farrell	Carpenter (as Pascall Farrell)
Paul Keogh	Carpenter
Daragh Lewis	Standby Props
Nuala McKernan	Chargehand Standby Props
Sunny Mulligan	Props Buyer
Owen Murnane	Master Painter
Tony Murnane	Standby Painter
Turlo Nicholson	Dressing Props
Eamonn O'Higgins	Property Master
Dave Peters	Dressing Props
John Purdy	Standby Rigger
Robbie Reilly	Chargehand Rigger
Gerard Richardson	Painter

Brian Thompson	Construction Runaround
Tony Walsh	Carpenter
Graham Waters	Standby Carpenter
Dave Whelan	Chargehand Carpenter
Mick Boggis	Sound Re-recording Mixer
Gordon Brown	Foley Editor
Brendan Deasy	Sound Mixer
Alan Douglas	Music Recordist
Jennie Evans	Digital Sound Editor
Peter Joly	Supervising Sound Editor
Danny Longhurst	Dialogue Editor
Peter Maxwell	Sound Re-recording Mixer
Máirín Ní Ríordáin	Trainee Sound
Trevor O'Connor	Sound Mixer: Winter Unit
Barry O'Sullivan	Boom Operator: Winter Unit
Eddie Quinn	Boom Operator
Steve Hancock	Sound Camera Operator (uncredited)
Graham Bushe	Special Effects Technician
Patrick Condren	Stunt Co-ordinator
Nigel Barker	Lightworks Assistant
Stephen Barker	Post-production Accountant
Ernie Beakhurst	Unit Driver
Dave Bronze	Musician: bass, Eric Clapton's band
Alison Byrne	Wardrobe Assistant (as Allison Byrne)
Frances Byrne	Production Co-ordinator (as Fran Byrne)
Sean Cahill	Electrician: Winter Unit
Stephen Carroll	Mechanic
Mary Casey	First Assistant Editor
John Cawley	Truck Driver
Tanya Cawley	Utility Stand-in
Eric Clapton	Musician: performer
Tony Cullen	Unit Driver
Richard Dann	Still Photo Processing
Lee Dickson	Guitar Technician: Eric Clapton's band
Noel Donnellon	Video Playback Operator
Sile Dorney	Cashier
Clare Doyle	Trainee Assistant Editor

Robbie Ellis	Mechanic
John Etherington	Grip
Penny Eyles	Script Supervisor
Andy Fairweather-Low	Musician: guitar, Eric Clapton's band
Jim Farrell	Best Boy Electric
Gerry Fearon	Transportation Captain
Steve Gadd	Musician: drums: Eric Clapton's band
Sally Ann Gately	Assistant Accountant
Donal Geraghty	Production Accountant
Liam Grant	Assistant Location Manager: Winter Unit
Rodrigo Gutierrez	Camera Operator (as Roderigo Gutierrez)
James Hagan	Trainee Clapper Loader
Celia Haining	Second Assistant Editor
Pippa Hall	Casting Assistant
Graeme Haughton	Electrician
Andrew Hegarty	Assistant Location Manager
Jonathan Hession	Still Photographer (as Jonathon Hession)
Billy Hinshelwood	Lawyer
Martin Holland	Generator Operator: Winter Unit
Allan Hughes	Grip: Winter Unit
Macdara Kelleher	Utility Stand-in
Austin Kelly	Wardrobe Truck Driver
Conor Kelly	Clapper Loader
Victor Keogh	Driver: Camera Car
Tommy Kingston	Driver: Set Property Truck
Bernadette Lovett	Production Secretary
Stephen McCarthy	Electrician
John McDonnell	Unit Location Manager
Rhona McGuirke	Wardrobe Supervisor
Ivan Meagher	Focus Puller
David Merrigan	Rigger
David Morris	Utility Stand-in
John Mulligan	Cashier: Winter Unit
Linda Murphy	Production Runner
Anne O'Halloran	Wardrobe Assistant
Keelin O'Síocháin	Trainee Costume Designer

Sian Parry	Assistant to Producer (as Sián Parry)
Jerry Portnoy	Musician: Harmonica, Eric Clapton's band
Larry S. Prinz	Gaffer (as Larry Prinz)
Michael Proudfoot	Camera operator: Winter Unit
Julian Rothenstein	Title Designer
Frank Ryan	Driver: Set Construction Truck
Kevin Scott	Generator Operator
Ravi Sharman	Drum Technician: Eric Clapton's band
Chris Stainton	Musician: Piano Organ, Eric Clapton's band
Francis Taaffe	Assistant Video Playback Operator (uncredited)

Bibliography

Barton, Ruth. *Irish National Cinema*. London: Routledge, 2004.

Bechmann, Helga. *Das Filmische Universum des Stephen Frears*. Alfeld/Leine: Coppi Verlag, 1997.

Beck, Ulrich, Natan Sznaider and Rainer Winter. Eds. *Global America?: the Cultural Consequences of Globalization*. Liverpool: Liverpool University Press, 2003.

Caherty, Therese. Ed. *Is Ireland a Third World Country?* Belfast: Beyond the Pale Publications, 1992.

Condren, Mary. *The Serpent and the Goddess: Women, Religion and Power in Celtic Ireland*. New York: Harper & Row, 1989.

Corcoran, Farrel. *RTÉ and the Globalisation of Irish Television*. Bristol: Intellect, 2004.

Crépon, Marc. 'Penser l'Europe avec Patočká. Réflexions sur l'altérité'. *Esprit*, No. 310 (December 2004): 27–42.

Cronin, Michael. 'Changing Times, Changing Cultures'. *Ireland and the European Union: The First Thirty Years, 1973–2002*. Ed. Jim Hourihane. Dublin: Lilliput Press, 2004. 12–25.

——. 'Moving Pictures: Kate O'Brien's Travel Writing', in *Ordinary People Dancing: Essays on Kate O'Brien*, ed. Eibhear Walshe. Cork: Cork University Press, 1993. 137–149.

——. *Translating Ireland*. Cork: Cork University Press, 1996.

Cronin, Seán. *Washington's Irish Policy: 1916–1986: Independence, Partition, Neutrality*. Dublin: Anvil Books, 1987.

Dolan, Terence. *A Dictionary of Hiberno-English*. Dublin: Gill & Macmillan, 1998.

Doyle, Roddy. *The Commitments*. Dublin: King Farouk, 1987.

——. *The Snapper*. London: Secker and Warburg, 1990.

——. *The Van*. London: Minerva, 1992.

Fay, Liam. 'Never Mind the Bollix!'. *Hot Press*, Vol. 17, No. 10 (1993): 39–40.

Gibbons, Luke. *The Quiet Man*. Cork: Cork University Press, 2002.

Gogan, Johnny. Review of *The Snapper*. *Film Ireland*, No. 35 (1993): 24.

Gray, Michael. *Stills, Reels and Rushes: Ireland and the Irish in Twentieth-Century Cinema*. Dublin: Blackhall, 1999.

Guckian, Brian. Review of *The Commitments*. *Film Base News*, No. 25 (1991): 18.

Hill, John, Martin McLoone and Paul Hainsworth. Eds. *Border Crossing: Film in Ireland, Britain and Europe*. Belfast: Institute of Irish Studies, 1994.

Inglis, Tom. *Moral Majority: the Rise and Fall of the Catholic Church in Modern Ireland*, second ed. Dublin: University College Dublin Press, 1998.

Kiberd, Declan. *Inventing Ireland*. London: Jonathan Cape, 1995.

Kirby, Peadar. *The Celtic Tiger in Distress: Growth with Inequality in Ireland*. London: Palgrave, 2002.

Lash, Scott, and John Urry. *Economies of Signs and Spaces*. London: Sage, 1994.

Leerssen, Joep. *Mere Irish and Fíor-Ghael: Studies in the Idea of Irish Nationality, its Development and Literary Expression Prior to the Nineteenth Century*. Amsterdam: John Benjamins, 1986.

Lothe, Jakob. *Narrative in Fiction and Film: an Introduction*. Oxford: Oxford University Press, 2000.

McCarthy, Conor. *Modernisation: Crisis and Culture in Ireland 1969–1992*. Dublin: Four Courts Press, 2000.

McCarthy, Dermot. *Roddy Doyle: Raining on the Parade*. Dublin: Liffey Press, 2003.

McKillop, James. Ed. *Contemporary Irish Cinema from* The Quiet Man *to* Dancing at Lughnasa. New York: Syracuse University Press, 1999.

McLoone, Martin. *Irish Film: the Emergence of a Contemporary Cinema*, London, British Film Institute, 2000.

Musser, Charles. 'The Travel Genre in 1903–1904: Moving Towards Fictional Narrative'. *Early Cinema: Space – Frame – Narrative*. Ed. Thomas Elsaesser. London: British Film Institute, 1990. 123–132.

Ó Dochartaigh, Niall. *From Civil Rights to Armalites: Derry and the Birth of the Irish Troubles*. Cork: Cork University Press, 1997.

Ó Gráda, Cormac. *The Economic Development of Ireland since 1870*. Dublin: Centre for Economic Research, UCD, 1993.

O'Connor, Barbara. 'Riverdance'. *Encounters with Modern Ireland*. Eds. Michel Peillon and Eamonn Slater. Dublin: IPA, 1998. 51–60.

O'Connor, Barbara and Michael Cronin. Eds. *Tourism in Ireland: a Critical Analysis*. Cork: Cork University Press, 1993.

O'Neill, Eithne. *Stephen Frears*. Paris: Rivages, 1994.

O'Toole, Fintan. 'Family Solidarity'. *Irish Times* (10 April 1993).

——. 'Going West: The Country Versus the City in Irish Writing'. *Crane Bag*, Vol. 9, No. 2: 111–116.

——. 'Working-Class Dublin on Screen: The Roddy Doyle Films'. *Cineaste*, Vol. 24, Nos. 2–3 (1999): 36–39.

——. *The Southern Question*. Dublin: Raven Arts Press, 1987.

Parker, Alan. 'Note'. The Tosser's Glossary. Press pack for *The Commitments* (1991).

——. 'Some Notes on the Making of the Film'. Production notes for *The Commitments* (1991).

——. 'The Making of *The Commitments*'. DVD. 20ᵗʰ Century Fox Home Entertainment (2000).

Parker, Alan. *Making Movies*. London: British Film Institute, 1998.

Patočká, Jan. *L'Idée de l'Europe en Bohême*. Trans. Erika Abrams. Grenoble: Jérôme Million, 1991.

Pettitt, Lance. *Screening Ireland: Film and Television Representation*. Manchester and New York: Manchester University Press, 2000.

Prendergast, Mark J. *Irish Rock: Roots, Personalities, Directions*. Dublin: O'Brien Press, 1987.

Rains, Stephanie. 'Home from Home: Diasporic Images of Ireland in Film and Tourism'. *Irish Tourism: Image, Culture and Identity*. Eds. Michael Cronin and Barbara O'Connor. Clevedon: Channel View Publications, 2003. 196–214.

Reynolds, Margaret. *Roddy Doyle*. London: Vintage, 2004.

Rockett, Kevin, Luke Gibbons and John Hill. *Cinema and Ireland*. New York: Syracuse University Press, 1988.

Rockett, Kevin. *Irish Film Censorship: a Cultural Journey from Silent Cinema to Internet Pornography*. Dublin: Four Courts Press, 2004.

Smyth, Gerry. *The Novel and the Nation: Studies in the New Irish Fiction*. London: Pluto, 1997.

Sweeney, Paul. *The Celtic Tiger: Ireland's Economic Miracle Explained*. Dublin: Oak Tree Press, 1998.

Taylor, Timothy D. 'Living in a Postcolonial World: Class and Soul in *The Commitments*'. *Irish Studies Review*, Vol. 6, No. 3 (1998): 291–302.

——. *The Commitments*. Production notes (1991).

——. *The Van*. Production notes (1996).

Thomson, David. *The New Biographical Dictionary of Film*. London: Little, Brown, 2002.

Titley, Gavan. *Youth Work with Boys and Young Men as a Means to Prevent Violence in Everyday Life*. Budapest: Council of Europe, 2003.

Vallely, Fintan. Ed. *The Companion to Irish Traditional Music*. Cork: Cork University Press, 1999.

Waters, John. *Jiving at the Crossroads*. Belfast: Blackstaff, 1991.

Waters, John. *Race of Angels: Ireland and the Genesis of U2*. Belfast: Blackstaff Press, 1994.

White, Caramine. *Reading Roddy Doyle*. New York: Syracuse University Press, 2001.